# ON HISTORY
# AND
# HISTORIOGRAPHY OF MANIPUR

# ON HISTORY
# AND
# HISTORIOGRAPHY OF MANIPUR

Gangmumei Kamei

**AKANSHA PUBLISHING HOUSE**
**NEW DELHI-110002**

**AKANSHA PUBLISHING HOUSE**
4649-B/21, Ansari Road
Darya Ganj, New Delhi - 110 002
Email: ektabooks@yahoo.com
Ph.: 23263193/9811582579
Fax: 011-23263193

ON HISTORY AND HISTORIOGRAPHY OF MANIPUR



First Published 2006
Reprint 2018

ISBN 81-8370-059-4



PRINTED IN INDIA

Published by M.P. Misra for Akansha Publishing House, New Delhi and Printed at Aryan Enterprises, Delhi

*Dedicated*
*to my respected father*
***Late Chanaphul Kamei,***
*a lover of knowledge and discipline*

# CONTENTS

# FOREWORD

It is a matter of great pleasure for me, both for intellectual and personal reasons to write foreword to Prof. Gangmumei Kamei's book *Philosophy of History and Historiography of Manipur.The* contents indicate the wide range of intellectual concerns covered by Kamei in the book. Many of these are of interest not only for the students of history but also for the students of anthropology and philosophy. I am glad that Kamei agreed to my amplifying some points so as to highlight the interdisciplinary character of his endeavour.

Earlier I had published a brief tract *Anthropology and History : Future of Past.* In my venture to amplify some of the points in Kamei's book, I had a quick second look at it, as well as at some of the books, I had gone through at that time and later. As I have freely drawn upon them, I should make a mention of some of the more important ones. *Indian Society: Historical Probing in memory of D.D. Kosambi* (ed.) R.S. Sharma; *The Problems of Philosophy*, Satischandra Chatterjee; *History of Western Philosophy*, Bertrand Russell; *Forecasting the Future*, Henry Winthrop; *A Vision of India's History*, Rabindranath Tagore; D.D. *Kosambi : On History and Society* (ed.) G. Syed; *The Past and Prejudice*, Romila *Thapar;Anthropology as a Historical Science* (ed.) Mahipal Bhuriya and S. M. Michael; *Explanation and Understanding in Human Sciences*, G. *Mahajan,Anthropology and History*, Evans Pritchard. I have also re-examined the chapter,"Issues in methodology" in my book, *Tribes in Perspective* and Kamei's earlier publication, *History of Manipur.I* am not mentioning here the well known philosophers of history, like Braudel, Collingwood, Meyerhoff or enthno-historiographers like Cohn andTrigger whom I had covered in my earlier write-up on *Anthropology and History*, and whose writings I have not re-examined on this occasion.

In writing about philosophy of history, I feel it necessary to try to understand what philosophy is all about. As mentioned by Kamei, "Collingwood regarded philosophy as a thought about thought". Clearly the title is towards intellectualism. For ancient Indian thinkers, philosophy is not merely an intellectual understanding of the truth, nor a matter of blind faith and unsteady belief. It is a direct knowledge or clear realisation of knowledge. This knowledge is to be attained through purification of the mind and contemplation of the self. It seems that Bertrand Russell's concept of philosophy in its wider sense, moves in the same direction. In his words, 'Philosophy is something intermediate between theology and science. like theology it consists of speculations on matters as to which definite knowledge has, so far been, unattainable, but like science, it appeals to human reason rather than to authority, whether that of tradition or that of revelation".

One may not be unjustifted in suspecting in this formulation traces of Locke's epistemological dualism. According to this the mind never directly perceives anything external to itself what it knows directly are its own states and processes-sensations, perceptions, images, ideas, etc. But from certain experiences of the mind, we can infer the existence of external objects as their causes. It is, however, difficult to say the sense-perception, whether internal or by itself external, gives us knowledge about reality, including the reality of historical process. But philosophy is not also mere initiative experience of reality. For many thinkers, particularly ancient Indian thinkers, philosophy is a combination of experience, reasoning and contemplation. This, in its turn, implies that reason *per se*, is not a way of knowing facts, but a way of rationalising or systematising our knowledge or facts. In this perspective, the dichotomy between scientiftc concept of philosophy and the concept of metaphysics or the study of reality as distinguished from appearances is very much reduced, if not obliterated. It is in this perspective that Collingwood's idea of metaphysics as a historical science of the absolute presuppositions of scientiftc thought at any period of history assumes its signiftcance.Again this provides a key for transaction of philosophy of history to the realm of science filtered through metaphysics. What, however, is not generally noticed in this transaction, is that science itself is partly relieved of its Baconean load and acquires a qualitative humanist hue. Perhaps, this provides a way out of the difficulty that Bertrand Russell faced in defining philosophy.

As noted by Kamei, according to Collingwood, philosophy of history is the enquiry into the special philosophical problem created by the existence of organised and systematised historical research. This apparently posits two operational strategies for a practitioner of historical research. One operational strategy is to carry out "organised and historical research" according to the methodology of historiography and then delve into the philosophical implications of the output of the historical research.The other operational strategy is to ingrain the essence of philosophy in the historical research method itself. Collingwood, as distinct from the Positivists, has opted for the second strategy. "All history is re-enactment in the historian's mind of the thought whose history he is studying". But how does this reenactment take place? This is a problem common to modern ethnography and history and perhaps to all the human sciences. According to Chinese Taoist philosophy, the highest attainment of man is the identification of man himself with the reality of things. This identity is not a concept of mediation or rational synthesis of the subjectivity of man and the objectivity of things. It is the direct spontaneous mutual solution which takes place at the absolute moment in his approach, rooted in ontology provides a backdrop for philosophy of history; but it is difficult to operationalise in historiographical research.

From critical realistic perspective, Herbert Read suggests, "We see what we want to see, and what we want to see is determined not by inevitable laws of optics, or even by an instinct for survival, but by the desire to discover or construct a credible world" .This is reflected in the Euro-centric writing of the Western philosophers during the dawn of the colonial era. It was none other than the great philosopher Hume, who wrote in 1748, "I am apt to suspect the Negroes, and in general for all other species of man ( for there are four or five different species) to be naturally inferior to the whites". Then again in his observations on the beautiful and sublime, Kant (1764) claims that the fundamental difference between the black and the white races of man appears to be as great in regard to mental capacities as in colour. And yet Kant was a philosopher of the sublime. Hegel, echoing Hume and Kant, claimed that Africans had no history, because they had developed no system of writing and had not mastered the art of writing in European languages. Levy Bruhl tried to establish the impossibility of philosophical dialogue and obvious non-existence of a tradition of organised philosophical system among the peoples of Africa. As against these great seers of the colonial era, Asike, a contemporary African scholar writes about the philosophical sagacity that permeates the world-view of the African peoples.

The feasibility for re-enactment in the historian's mind, the thought of those who are being studied may perhaps be derived from some of the anthropological traditions.

The Hermeneutic theory of the nineteenth century often spoke of the circular structure of understanding, but always within the framework of a formal relation of the part and the whole or its subjective reflex, the intuitive anticipation of the whole and its subsequent articulation in the parts. According to this theory, the circular movement of understanding runs backwards and forwards along with the text and disappears when it is perfectly understood. As against this approach Heidegger describes the circle in such a way that the understanding of the text remains permanently determined by the anticipatory movement of fore-understanding. The circle is neither subjective nor objective but describes understanding as the interplay of the movement of tradition and the movement of the interpreter. The anticipation of the meaning that governs our understanding of a text is not an act of subjectivity but proceeds from the communality that binds us to tradition.

Hermeneutic understanding is close to Husserl's phenomenological approach. In his philosophical system neutral field of consciousness or 'intuition essence'is a priori self evident and may also be prelogical. Here, the concept of prelogical does not imply 'illogical' .What Husserl means is that the principles categorising Western thought may not be present in the thinking of the entities under study.

Drawing upon Herber and other theorists in the same wave length, Mahajan begins with the assumption that when we choose a particular mode of explanation or understanding an object, we construct the object differently from the ones that are not chosen. Apart from hermeneutic understanding, the modes chosen by us are causal explanation, reason-action-explanation and narration. Underlying causal explanation is the belief generally held by social scientists, that the nature of reality is based on order rather than chaos and that much of this order has to do with cause and effect sequences among phenomena that he cannot scientifically prove with certainty that any given relationship among phenomena is one of cause and effect. Because of this, he may not even use the terms 'cause and affect' in his communications; instead he talks about relationship among variables. Mahajan has drawn attention to another dimension of causal explanation. Several theorists suggest that linking together of two variable objects points to the existence of a law which may or may not remain unstated. But they argue that it follows from a covering law-model, and that a successful prediction is an attribute of a scientific explanation. It, however, seems that those who hold this view fail to differentiate between prediction and prophecy. Prediction implies a perception of probability, prophecy implies a claims of certainty. While predictions in social sciences have a lower probability of success, than those in physical sciences, this by itself cannot be a ground to abandon the causal relation enquiry. At the same time, this cannot be the only mode of approach to reality. One of the others, is reason-action explanation. In this framework actions are distinguished from events and intentionality is the distinctive attribute. This approach assumes that historical agents are rational persons; they choose a particular cause of action because they feel that this would enable them to pursue and realise their goals, desires and interests. One of the pitfalls in this approach is that it fails to take note of the role of subconscious in the reason-action-paradigm.

The narrative mode upholds a series of happenings about an identifiable and determinate objects. Reference to one continuous object provides coherence to the story and offers basis for indentifying all those incidents that are relevant for explaining the event. As distinct from chronicle, it presents every event in the series as a consequence of the mediation of the action of different agents.The difficulty in this approach is that "consequence " tends to be assumed on a single causal basis. In such situations many would argue in favour of multi-variant analysis, but this means complete rejection of phenomenological approach. Which is associated with the humanist engagement of the researcher with his own self. In this context hermeneutic understanding all already discussed becomes relevant.

But hermeneutic understanding presupposes 'psychic unity of mankind' as postulated by many thinkers even in the ancient ages and reaffirmed in anthropology by Bastian in the late 19th century and by Evans Pritchard and others in recent decades. Structuralism of Levi Strauss has elaborated it with great sophistication.

In Straussian framework, societies differ from one another just as their surface grammars differ but there is a deep common. Levi Strauss believes that basic thinking occurs as sets of contrasts; day and night; black and white; life and death. Such dualism shows up in the superstructure in various ways, for instance, in moiety organisation and in myths. What is, however, important to note is that Strauss does not see deep structures as determinative and causal but as providing surface variety. Though there are universal deep structures, cultures are also moulded by their physical and social environment. Obviously, Strauss prefers to be cautious and draws an intellectual rabicon line. But Leach does not have any hesitation to cross the rabicon line and speak of "inspired guess work".

Consciously or unconsciously, many historians go in for 'inspired guess work". But then one has to win the hurdle race of establishing the authenticity. Truth and error are characters of judgements or propositions which are verbal expressions of judgements.To establish the authenticity of the understanding of a historical event or historical situation, the pertinent questions are: how truth and error are constituted and how they are known or tested. Chatterjee suggests, that there are four main theories of truth and error which bear on these two questions. These are known as the intuitionist, the coherence, the pragmatist and the correspondence theories of truth and error.

According to the intutionist theory, while truth is intrinsic to one kind of knowledge, error or falsity is intrinsic to a different kind. Such assertion that one is seeing two moons in the sky can be immediately invalidated as a statement of error; but judgement about truth remains problematic. Subjective certitude or consciousness of objectivity as such, cannot be accepted as a test of truth.

There are two main schools, namely, Logical Positivists and Hegelians holding the test of coherence. To realists coherence as a criteria of truth may mean the agreement of one kind of experience with those of a different kind, or it may mean consistency of one belief of judgement or proposition with other so as to form a system. The idea of samvada which is accepted as a test of truth by some Indian logicians brings out the first sense of coherence as agreement among different kinds of experiences. Thus, the visual perception of an object is found to be true when it coheres with, i.e., agrees with the tactual and other kinds of perception of the same object. The other idea of coherence as a logical consistency of beliefs or judgements in a system is endorsed by Bertrand Russell, L. T. Hobhouse and others. But Russell qualifies his acceptance of the test of coherence by stating that while it increases probability, it can never be given absolute certainty, unless there is certainty already at some point in the coherence system.

Hobhouse is in the same wavelength as this approach and calls it 'consilience'. According to him validity below to judgement as forming a consilient system.

In Hegelian form of coherence theory, a system of thought may be formally consistent but materially false, and therefore, not true. For them truth in its essential nature is that systematic coherence which is the character of a significant whole, and significant whole as an organised individual experience, self fulfilling and self fulfilled. This, however, implies a process, which is dialectical in character. When an entity or event appears the thesis appears; it is countered by the emergence of its opposite-the antithesis. The conflict between the two resolves itself as a synthesis, which, taking some elements of both thesis and anti thesis elevates both, bringing about a new and higher event. In turn synthesis becomes thesis, is negated again by its antithesis, resolving again in a new synthesis.The measure of historical truth lies in the grasp of this process. The historical event, although irreversible and autonomous, can nevertheless be placed in its dialectic, which remains open but at the same time conforms to the plan of providence. Hence 'it has a model in the dialectics of spirit itself and the dialectical method of Hegel stands or falls with its fundamental assumption that thought and reality are identical. This would have been true, if when we think of anything the thing alw. ys comes into existence. This criticism does not completely deny the role of idea in history; but it is obvious that coherence between idea and reality as in Hegelian framework is of limited validity. The pragmatist theory of truth and error is advocated by William James, E.C.S. Schiller, John Dewey and others. James postulates that an idea becomes true in so far as it leads to certain experiences which verify it and it is useful in so far as the experiences it leads to fulfil its function in one's actual life. In other words for James, truths are processes which possess only one common quality, namely, they pay. In Schiller's theory 'true' is the term for the positive value of successful prediction and is opposed to falsity which is the negative value of a failure to predict. Pierce who first introduced the word 'pragmatism' defmes truth as follows: "The opinion which is fated to have been ultimately agreed to by all who investigate is what we mean by truth and object represented by this opinion is real". This means that truth is the ideal which we are to attain by endless scientific investigation and that a particular statement or proposition is true in so far as it is provisionally established by investigation.

Dewey's theory of truth agrees in the main with that of Pierce. But he prefers the words 'warranted assertibility' for knowledge or truth. The pragmatists are not satisfied by the agreement between our ideas and their corresponding cognitive experiences. They insist further on the agreement of the ideas with such other experiences as result from our activities in relation to the objects represented by the ideas. It has been criticised by many that in actual life situation, this approach, reduces "the true" to "the useful" and thereby obliterates the distinction between truth and error.

The correspondence theory exists in many forms. First the old school of common-sense or naive realism, according to which truth and that all our normal perceptions are true in this sense. But if every knowledge or experience reveals objects as they really are, we cannot explain how different persons perceive differently as sometimes opposite qualities in the same thing at the same time.

The theory of naive or natural realism with correspondence notion of truth is presented in a modified form by new-realism. Some of the new realists suppose that there is a structural identity between the content of knowledge and the object known. They adopt a searchlight view of consciousness and speak of it as a cross section of reality. Just as a searchlight by playing over a landscape and illuminating its different parts makes a separate section of them from other parts not so illuminated, so consciousness is the cross section or collection of objects illuminated by it and the things themselves become contents of knowledge. This approach involves an element of selection in the focus of the searchlight or in other words in the "attention" of the consciousness. One may, however, ask whether it is a matter of accident or is determined by some agent?

The question of determination will be addressed to separately. As regards new-realist theory of correspondence, it is criticised that even if it is true in case of visual and tactual images, it hardly holds good in case of other kinds of images and far less of ideas and percepts.

Modern critical realism approaches the correspondence theory of truth from a different vantage point. According to it there are three distinct factors in any knowledge, namely, mental state, data and object. The data of knowledge are the character complexes through which the object is presented to the mind. In case of some data only (i.e. those presenting primary qualities), we may say that they are in a sense the character of things or objects. Knowledge is true in so far as it corresponds to its objects in the sense that the character complexes through which the objects are known are identical with the real characters of those objects. But in complex historical situations, the data may be incomplete, may be perceived out of context and in such cases the knowledge may be erroneous.

There are also other types of correspondence theory of truth, relevant for historical research method. According to one, truth of knowledge means its correspondence to some experience; according to another it consists in its correspondence to some fact which may or may not be experienced. The first is called 'epistemological' and the second, the 'logical' theory of correspondences.

According to epistemological theory, a judgement is true when it agrees with given facts or experiences, and false when it fails to do so. Against this formulation it is argued that if the truth of a judgement consists in its correspondence, not to an independent object, but to a mere presentation, then even an illusion will have to be regarded as true knowledge, since there is in it an actual presentation of the illusory object.

The logical theory of correspondence is advocated by Bertrand Russell. According to him a proposition is true when it corresponds with some real occurrence or fact. There seems to be a parallel in logical realism of Nyaya school of Indian philosophy. The Nyaya believes in an independent facts. According to it, the truth of knowledge consists in its correspondence with objective facts, while coherence and practical utility are the tests of truth in such cases in which we require a rest. It defines truth of all knowledge as correspondence of relations.

While truth consists in correspondence, the criterion of truth is, for Nyaya, coherence in a broad sense. But coherence here is different from what objective idealism projects. The Nyaya coherence is a practical test and means the harmony between cognitive and conative experiences or between different kind of knowledge.

There is a point of view that different theories of truth as discussed may be shown to supplement one another. Perhaps this is possible, if as Mandelshohn suggests, exchange and amalgam of elements of different propositions and perspectives is effected. An outstanding example of this is antagonistic amalgam of elements of Hegelian idealistic dialectics and dialectical materialism of Marx.

Marx found in Hegelian dialectics, a frame, which from the opposite end, could be used for materialist appreciation of history. Dialectic materialist analysis tries to demonstrate that the production of the means of existence exercises a determining influence upon all other human activities, thus conditioning social, political and spiritual processes as a whole. It is in this sense that the production by men of the material conditions of their life is the tool of history. In producing material goods, people simultaneously produce themselves as social individuals, as the result of their productive activity is always, not only use values, material and spiritual values, but society itself, man himself as bearer of social being. For this reason, the history of the development of social production is always the history of social development of individuals, their own history, and vice versa. Dialectics enter into the process through mismatch between means of production and relations of production leading to relentlees struggle for new equation. From Marxist perspective Kosambi observes, "History is the presentation in chronological order of successive changes in the means and relations of production."

Dialectical materialism is misinterpreted by many to mean economic determinism; but on this, Engel's letter to J. Block written in 1890 should have served as the corrective. In the words of Engels, "According to the materialist conception of history, the ultimately determining element in history is the production and reproduction of real life. More than this neither Marx nor I have even asserted".

Hence if somebody twists this into saying that the economic element is the only determining one, he transforms that proposition into a meaningless abstract, senseless phrase". In the same letter Engels gave great importance to political forms, constitution, juridical forms, religious views also. This in a way envisages the importance of the history of specific social entities (Marxo-history) in grasping the process of transformation of mega-social formation.The term more in currency is ethno-history rather than micro-history. I would have gone in for the term micro-history. But as Kamei has used the term ethnohistory in his book, I am sticking to the same in the Foreword to the book to avoid confusion. Ethno historical enquiry is not only related to the probe into the subaltern life-scape but is related to the totality of human life scape. History of humanity is, in the long run, indivisible, ethno-history in isolation is mutilation of history.

Trigger has observed that of late ethno-historians are turning to anthropology for fulftlment of some of their professional requirements. He, however, makes a distinction between ethno-historians and conventional historians. Ethno-historians habitually rely more than conventional historians, upon oral traditions and other sources of data, such as archaeology, historical linguistics, physical anthropology and comparative ethnology to supplement the written records.

B.S. Cohn further differentiates between ethno-historian and colonial historian. Usually ethno-historian has first hand field experience, knowledge of indigenous society and its functions; thinks in systematic functional terms, rather than in terms of accidents and particulars, uses his general knowledge of social and cultural organisation and constructs his units in terms of such concepts as 'segmentary lineage based society', 'peasant society', 'patrimonial society', tries to perceive historical events from position of the indigenous peoples, rather than of administrators and is more interested in the impact of colonial policy and practice than in the genesis of these policies in the metropolitan society.

This differentiation between ethno-historian and colonial historian by Cohn while reflecting the perspective or cultural pluralism, seems to be rather too formal in appreciating the meaning of history. While ethno-historian will have to give primacy to the non dominant indigenous point to view and to the micro context in its temporal depth, he need not confme himself to the micro-context only. Micro context in temporal depth is only the starting point, and in terms of this operational strategy, the so-called ethno-history is micro-history. But micro-context must not be ignored. Otherwise there would be hardly any difference between him and the colonial historian. For instance, one can take up the 19th century history of North East India, as presented by a colonial historian, Mackenzie and as presented recently in a historical monograph. Mackenzie had first prepared in 1869 a *Memorandum on the North East Frontier of Bengal*. Later in 1884 he brought out a revised publication, *History of relation of the government with the hill tribes of North East Frontier of British Bengal.The* shift in focus from one publication to the other is quite important. In the first one, the geo-political context of the colonial rule and its objective becomes important; in the second, one can completely ignore geo-political context and overall colonial commercial and strategic interest and project the relations of the government with the hill tribes as informed by altruistic intention of carrying out 'the white man's burden' against the backdrop of intertribal conflicts or antagonistic relations of the tribal peoples with Ahom rulers. In fact, this is exactly what Mackenzie had achieved in his second publication. Unaware of the over all colonial policy, not only many among tribal peoples agree with him, but as a recent historical research, under the aegis of a renowned Indian University shows, some non-colonial historians also agree with him. In the research publication referred to, an Assamese scholar had described the British administration in the early 19th century as revolutionary in character. Giving priority to the improvement of the general conditions of the people,Jenkins suggested,"it could be done by the operation of the land survey by ascertaining and fixing every man's possession and defming the demand of the government upon each individual". "The common people who were not involved in the resentment of the deprivation of rights and privileges of the nobility but had to suffer from a miserable life due to political turmoil, devastation caused by famine and economic oppression were naturally satisfied with the change of administration". After saying all these the scholar however admits that"a newly adopted measure of the European Government to impose tax on all kinds of lands including the waste lands and those so far considered as tax-free, created dissatisfaction among some people". Even than the scholar failed to take note of the fact that by this approach, vast tracts of communal lands were usurped as state land and a large area was leased out to tea-estates, most of which belonged to Europeans and another slice of large area was declared as state owned reserved forests. Chon's normative approach to ethno-history does not guard against this type of lapse. In fact some recent trends in ethno-history's concern seem to be moving in the direction of creating capsules of history for influencing the historical process.Wernhart, for instance, after stating that from the methodical point of view, ethno-history uses the historical method but in its interpretation it proves to be an ethnological discipline, convenes itself as structural history and tries to show by means of this research approach the cultural changes and development that have taken place in an ethnic group observes that ethno-history thus constructed is necessary for implementing same programmes of exogenous origin.

Such trends confirm the observation made earlier that Cohn has failed to take note of the dynamic aspect of history itself. As observed by Teggart, the contemporary historian presents only such matters as from his views are of importance. The historian sets out to create a whole and his whole is of necessity the organisation of a body of facts from the point of view of some a priori interest. In the philosophy of history, Meyerhoff mentions that value emotive meanings, ideological concepts invariably enter into the study of history. These are subject to change and social climate.

In the contemporary world, where macroscopic view of human situation is percolating all sections of society, this dynamic perception of the meaning of history has also been discussed by Kamei in the present book as a corrective against universalising the particularistic "Universal" of the West.

It is obvious that there is no unchanging past. With shift in the focus of interest in the world view of peoples the contour of the past will go on changing.The future of the past is thus a continuous present. With a slightly different reasoning Evans Pritchard presents a similar view. He distinguishes the effect of one event from the memory of the event. As memory is socially selective, perception of the past goes on changing. Proceeding further Pritchard observes that, perhaps it is in this sense that Croce had stated that all history is contemporary history.

In the second part of the book Kamei has discussed in considerable detail the historiography of Manipur with particular focus on the life history of Meitei polity. He mentions that traditional Meitei concept of history is expressed by the Meitei word *puwari* (story of forefathers).

An interesting fact of historiography of Manipur was that the person who is believed to be the first historical *king,Pakhangba,* was preceded by the divine Pakhangbas, but the historical Pakhangba was not originally claimed to be divine. Divinity was later imputed to him.The time of Pakhangba's reign is ascribed by some to 33 A.D. But others to 3rd/4th century A.D. It was only on the mid-17th century, that Khagemba, indisputably claimed divine kingship of Manipur.These two flash points in Manipur's history are worth being reflected upon.

Here it may not be irrelevant to recall what Machiavelli stated in *The Prince.* Kingdoms known to history have been governed in two ways: either by a prince and his servants, who as ministers by his grace and permission against in governing the real realm, or by a prince and by barons, who hold their positions not by favour of the ruler but by antiquity of blood" .These are two pure types of kingdom organised on patrimonial principle and feudal principle. But in actual historical situation there would be various permutations and combinations of elements of these two principles. In Manipur there has been always permutations and combinations of elements of these principles and the shifting permutations and combinations, are along with other things, related to changes in the boundary of the kingdom as well as to the changes in the social composition of the peoples brought in subordinate relation to the king, either as direct subjects or as subsidiary allies or as tribute paying population through the straps recognised by the king.

It seems that after passing through a phase of confederacy of extremely localised polities, Pakhangba succeeded to establish a patrimonial kingdom with a limited jurisdiction. For a long time the fiat of his successors also did not cover the whole of Imphal valley. Around the later part of 11th century, when the Ningthouja King Taothing Mang a distant successor of Pakhangba attempted to cross Angom territory, to help his brother in irrigation work, he was challenged by an Angom archer of Funan village for trespassing into their territory. The king was injured by an arrow of the archer and the place where it happened was called Nganglau (blood-red place). It was only expansion of the jurisdiction of the kingdom through conquests by successive kings involving twist and turns strain to the pluralistic ethos, cherished by the people. Historiography is not mere method of history; historiography is also a vacuum cleaner of history

Prof. B.K. Roy Burman

Chittaranjan Park,
New Delhi

# INTRODUCTION

**On History and Historiography of Manipur** is an anthology of research papers on different aspects of the historical method and regional historiography of north–east India and Manipur written at different times. These papers deals with the analysis of the historical philosophy, historical method and different aspects of historiography concerning Manipur. There are a couple of papers on interpretation of history. This book was earlier published by Manipur University Research Club where the members were the research scholars. And the circulation was more or less limited to the research scholars. The earlier title was "Philosophy of History and Historiography of Manipur" (1997). There are many requests from friends that the work may be reissued. The original publishers, the research scholars belonging to different academic disciplines are now well established in their professions. Professor N. Joykumar Singh, Director, Centre for Manipur Studies of Manipur University took the initiative for the present publication for which I thank him with a sense of satisfaction and gratitude.

I would like to reproduce an extract from the preface to the earlier publication in which I wrote, "History and Historical studies have been my life long profession. Now history has become a highly theoretical academic discipline. It is now recognized as a social science with all its ramifications. It has been a convergence of circumstances that I could come with contact with some of the brilliant minds of the country, leading histrorians, anthropologists, sociologists, economists and men of letters. As a social activist, I have been exposed to the complex realities of a plural society like Manipur. These two exposures strengthen my academic roots. And I have learnt a lot from the indigenous social laboratory of Manipur. I have tried to apply the multi-disciplinary approach in tackling several research problems including historical issues. As a student of history, I have always tried to understand the meaning, significance, concept, method and interpretation of history. The papers of the volume were earlier published in different journals. Sometimes, these papers will appear lacking cohesion, and not having a comprehensive and systematic exposition on philosophy and historiography."

I express my gratefulness to the past research scholars for engaging me to formulate my thoughts on the historical problems and social science research issues when I was teaching History in Manipur University. I would like to mention the names of Dr. L. Bishwanath Sharma of Philosophy Department of Manipur University, K. Jitendra Sharma, L. Gojendra and Mrs. N. Nalini for their help.

I have retained the highly illuminating metaphysical foreword to this book, written by Professor B.K. Roy Burman for which I am extremely grateful to him. I thank Shri Nilmani Singh, Shri A. Kamei and Dr. Ram Kamei for the cover design

I am also thankful to Shri M.P. Misra, the proprietor of Akansha Publishing House, New Delhi for publishing this book at a short notice.

Imphal
11th April, 2006

Gangmumei Kamei

## CHAPTER ONE

# PHILOSOPHY OF HISTORY

### What is philosophy of history?

What is the philosophy of history? Is there a philosophy of history? These two questions have been engaging the minds of the philosophers since the eighteenth century, while practising historians do not give attention to this metaphysical issue of history. The term, "Philosophy of History" was first coined by the famous Enlightenment philosopher of France, Voltaire who is regarded as the best representative of the Age of Reason and the rationalist resurrection against the orthodox theological Christian historiography of the middle ages. Can there be a branch of philosophy known as the philosophy of history? Patrick Gardiner, a Cambridge philosopher thinks that it is 'misleading' to speak of philosophy of history as a single branch of academic studies and nor the philosophy of history can be defined in the conventional sense.

However, philosophers of three different schools, the Rationalist Voltaire, the Idealist Hegel and the Positivist Auguste Comte thought that the philosophy of history was a matter of metaphysical speculation and its aim was to attain an understanding of the course of history as a whole. Voltaire used the term "Philosophy of History" to convey the idea of a critical and scientific history as distinct or differentiated from the Christian theological interpretation of history which was current in Europe since the early middle ages. It requires a philosopher of Voltaire's scholarship, repute and influence to stand up against the Christian historiography with its strong belief in the divine providence as the motive force of history. Voltaire was a versatile writer; while his views were respected by his contemporaries, he did not develop any detailed systematic thought. He did not explain the philosophy of history in detail though he wrote several books of history.

It was Hegel who developed his concept of philosophy of history in his famous *"Lectures on Philosophy of History"* (1822-24). Hegel was the foremost philosopher of early nineteenth century and his views were accepted in the philosophical world of western Europe. His philosophy of history was a part of his philosophical system. To Hegel the idea or reason is the motive force of universal history or cosmic change. It develops in a dialectical process according to which one idea or proposition which he calls thesis is posed against another proposition which produces an antithesis, out of which emerges a proposition which is common to both the opposing propositions in the form of a synthesis. Hegel believes that dialectic is the process of expression of the idea or motive force in history. The highest form of expression of the idea or reason is the emergence of the institution of the State. Hegel almost deified the State which he called the March of God on earth. And his philosophy of history is taken as a thinking about the world as a whole, of course, in simple language, it is also a critical and scientific appreciation of the process of change which ultimately would lead to the supremacy of the State. Hegel raised the speculation on history as a distinct branch of philosophy.

Auguste Comte of France who founded the Positivist School of thought, gave a great importance to the study of history. He applied the philosophy of history to mean the discovery of the general laws governing the course of events in history and working of different institutions and phenomena in social systems. The Positivist interpretation of history gave a general impetus to the study of history throughout Europe. Study of history became quite popular in the nineteenth century; and the Positivists tried to build up another discipline known as sociology out of the historical data. But this school committed a folly of ignoring the fact that history was already an autonomous academic discipline. However, their attempt to discover the uniform laws governing societies and social activities of men added a dimension to the philosophy of history and made it a branch of social sciences.

Of all the modem philosophers and historians, a credit should be given to the English philosopher and historian of Oxford, R. G. Collingwood who gave the first exposition of the philosophy of history which has come to mean a systematic interpretation of the universal history in accordance with the principle by which the historical events and succession are unified and directed towards an ultimate meaning. Collingwood observes, philosophy of history does not consist in speculation on the course of the historical events in toto, nor is it an attempt to formulate and justify historical generalisations upon which prediction of future events can be based. Philosophy of history is properly an attempt to elucidate the special nature of historical reasoning and historical knowledge, in short, an attempt to answer the question, "What is history ?" Then it will cover all issues of historical method, namely, definition of history, objective of historical studies, nature of history, objectivity, conceptualisation, periodization, selection of and authenticity of sources of information etc.

## Historical determinism: Purpose of history

What is the purpose of history? Modem philosophers and historiographers do not attribute any purpose for history, or determinism in history. However, historical determinism was strongly emphasised by theological historiographers specially by the writers of Christian historiography and the protagonists of the pre-deterministic political and social ideologies like Marxism. Christian theological historiography strongly emphasised that the purpose of history which proceeds according to the divine plan is the ultimate realisation of the eternal will of God for spiritual redemption of man or punishment of man in the hands of God. For Hegel, the dialectical idealism means that the ultimate reality of historical development was the realisation of the idea or reason to be manifested in the creation of the greatest institution of man known as the State. Hegelian philosophy, thus, aims at the glorification of the absolutist state. While his ultimate political philosophy was not tenable, the dialectical method applied by Karl Marx in the analysis of the evolution of human civilization or socio-economic system from the primitive communism to slave based empire and to Feudalism, to Capitalism and ultimately to Communism. Marx predicted that human society would ultimately culminate into the establishment of a classless, stateless society, living in the village communes where man will live according to his needs and without encroaching on others' properties or interests. The communist society has been pronounced as the ultimate aim of history. But such historical determinism is not unanimously accepted in historiography.

### St. Augustine: History as a divine plan

We may examine the Christian historiography of the middle ages represented by St. Augustine as a type of historical determinism St. Augustine was the greatest thinker of Christian political philosophy and the Christian historiography of the medieval age. It has been suggested that medievalism began with St. Augustine. Christianity had destroyed paganism. Roman empire had accepted

Christianity as its official religion; and Christianity had given a religious unity to Europe. St. Augustine lived in a period (354-430 AD.) which was an extremely critical for Christianity because of the Barbarian attacks on Rome. Alaric I and Visigoths sacked Rome in 410 AD. The destruction of the city of Rome and many things which Roman civilisation stood for appeared to be completed. There was a great debate, why the city of Rome was destroyed. Why did the Roman empire decline? Many non Christian leaders and writers attributed the fall of Rome to the acceptance of Christianity by Roman empire. Rome under the protection of her ancient gods had grown up from a mere city state to a world wide empire. Rome threw away its ancient religion, and Christianity had brought ruin to Rome. Many lamented that Christianity could not save Rome from destruction. The criticism of this kind provoked St. Augustine to take up the defence of Christianity. And he wrote his famous classic, De Civitate Dei (The City of God) in 22 volumes between 413-426 A.D. The first ten volumes were devoted to the defence of Christianity and the remaining 12 volumes to the explanation of the City of God.

St. Augustine developed the concept of Eternal Will of God to explain the historical development of the world. The fall of Rome was the part of the divine plan to create a new city of God on Earth. According to St. Augustine, God had ordained order, regularity and beauty in nature; and the story of mankind depends not upon chance but upon the eternal will of the Creator. There is a divine will behind everything. The history of mankind was a struggle between the forces of evil and forces of good. The forces of the evil were represented by the secular empires. But they were non permanent and they must give place to the City or kingdom of God. Thus, Augustine and following him Christian thinkers adopted a purely theological approach to history writing. They composed an Universal history based on the

Old Testament and the New Testament. They adopted a single chronological frame based on the birth of Jesus Christ as the historical sheet anchor; period before Christ and after Christ. A prominent place was given to the idea of providence in the evolution of human history which is predestined to be redeemed or punished by God; heaven or hell was the ultimate goal of man. This providential theory of Christian historiography dominated European historiography for several centuries till the coming of the historiography of the Rationalist school in the 18th century. This is a classic example of historical determinism in historiography. God as a Creator of the Universe and Maker of empires and nations, is accepted in the oriental countries. Though the theological approach has now been discarded by the scientific historians, some are still clinging to it.

**Development of the philosophy of history**

Collingwood observes that the philosophy of history had developed *pari passu* with the development of history itself. This implies that the philosophy of history is developed and is expected to follow a course parallel to the development of the historical knowledge. In the early period of human civilisation, the historical knowledge was in a rudimentary form, naturally the idea of the philosophy of history must have been in a crude form or even non existent. With the emergence of historical knowledge as an organised and complex discipline, it has evolved its own methodology and philosophy. Collingwood and other scientifc historians outright dismissed that none of the ancient historians had developed any philosophy of history. At the same time, we have to remember that the concept of historiography of a particular period is the reflection of the historical knowledge attained by the historians of the period. Therefore, in the Greco-Roman period, the historians more or less adopted the method of writing history based on the available source of information. The Greco-Roman historiography which was a superior one was abandoned by the Christian historiography whieh adopted as explained in the previous paragraphs by the theological method to explain and predict the ultimate victory of Christianity. We have explained the inadequacies of historical determinism in the ideas of St. Augustine. It has been claimed by many modern philosophers and historians that there is no philosophy of history in the writings of St. Augustine and other Christian writers. Perhaps they are right, but it must be stated that the scientific study of history or idea of the history of philosophy was developed as an antidote to or an escape from Christian theological historiography or historical determinism of Christianity.

**Scientific method**

In modern times, a philosophy of history was gradually evolved with philosophers raising the question, what is history? We may mention Giambattista Vico (1688-1744) of Italy who laid the foundation of the philosophy of history by adopting the scientific method in his writings particularly *The New Science.* According to Vico, historical knowledge cannot be poured out of one mind to another, it has to be built by each historian for himself using the universal and necessary principles of historical thought to interpret the historical data which the past had left behind. Vico also developed the cyclical theory of history according to which nations passed through certain stages of change, rise, maturity, decline and fall, Vieo still believed in the providence ordained by God as the basis of historical development. he made innovations in the historical method; in the first place, the importance of study of language (Etymology); second, use of the myths and mythology in the reconstruction of history; third, use of tradition which represented, according to him, a confused memory of faith; and fourth, an analysis of the growth process of old societies, Vico contributed a liberating methodology for the reconstruction of cultural history.

## Leopold von Ranke

With the Enlightenment, history was liberated from the grip of theology. In the beginning of 19th Century, Hegel's dialectic and his speculation on history were accepted by the generations of philosophers. His philosophy of history gained great respectability in philosophical circle. At the sametime, in Germany a very scientific and critical school of history based on empiricism was developed by the great historian Leopold von Ranke (1795-1886). Ranke and his school of historians dominated history writing in Europe. Ranke followed and developed a methodology earlier adopted by a German scholar Reinhold Neibuhr. As observed by Marwick, "by the intensive application of critical technique, by sheer industry, and pertinacious research, was a new and more refined historical methodology created. Eventually the primacy of the original source could become an excuse for perpetrating the most tiresome pedantries; but is in doing so imperatively a dedication to the critical use of primary materials to a profound scale of historical change, Leopold von Ranke performed an inestimable service to historical studies which justly entitled him to be regarded as the founder of modern discipline of history." Ranke also tried to divorce the study of past from the passion of the present. He insisted that the strict presentation of facts is the supreme law of historical writing. He also played a significant role in the teaching of history at the University level through his seminars at the University of Berlin. He published the first historical journal, *Historische Zeischrift* containing true method of historical research. Ranke also developed the science of evidence of historiography. He has been hailed as the greatest historian of the 19th century.

## Decline of philosophy of history

In the later part of 19th century, despite Karl Marx's materialist intpretation of history as a tenet of communism, the interest in Philosophy of history had declined because of the growth of vast historical knowledge of the individual historian, which was the legacy of Ranke. In the beginning of 20th century, eminent historians with the original knowledge of historical methodology started a scientific study of history both at the universal and the national levels. Lord Acton in Britain, Benedetto Croce in Italy, Oswald Spengler in Germany interpreted history based on the historical knowledge of the individual historian. Spengler's *The Decline of* the *West* is a modern application of the theory of cyclical change in history explaining that the West in the beginning of 20th century had declined. Spengler did not have many supporters but the method of his presentation was very fresh. Spengler did not have popularity after his death.

## Philosophy of history means historical method

It is not proposed to dwell into the thoughts of several great historians in their philosophy of history or historical methodology. But it has now been universally agreed that philosophy of history means more or less the historical method. Credit should be given to R.G. Collingwood who had with his very sharp and logical mind and wide knowledge for explaining and developing the concept of philosophy of history. The philosophy of history has nothing to do with cosmic plan of the Divine Will behind historical development as developed by St. Augustine, nor is it a manifestation of reason as propounded by the writers of the Idealist School of thought. True, scholars like Eretrand Russell, Arnold J. Toynbee still believe in the interplay of reason and theology in the evolution of universal history. However, hard-headed schclars like E.H. Carr fully agree with Collingwood that philosophy of history means the answer to the question, what is history? Hence philosophy o^f history is the historical method.

CHAPTER TWO

# REASON AND HISTORICAL REASONING

## An Analysis of the Historical Method

### Reason and Reasoning

There is no universally accepted sense of reason. The philosophers give different opinions. In common parlance, reason is a faculty of power of intelligent and disappasionate thought; it is also regarded as a basis, a circumstance explaining some belief, action, fact and event. And the faculty of reason is a special talent peculiar to man who has the capacity to think. Reason is defined as 'the faculty and function of grasping the necessary connection.' Reason can be better understood if it is related to knowledge and experience. The scope of reason covers the whole field of knowledge and inquiry in which men produce or seek reasons for their view, proof, evidence and explanation for their conclusion and ground for their conclusion. Reason ultimately is an explanation for certain action; reason and cause are inter related. There is a linkage between reason and causation of action.

Reasoning is the process of the faculty to perceive truth or arrive at the truth. Reason and reasoning are essentially the processes of arriving at and situating the truth in a phenomenon. Reason in a way is equivalent to thinking which is a mental activity to attain knowledge and find the truth. Therefore, reasoning is a mental act of a person who reasons or the process of forming conclusion, judgement or inference from facts or premises. Reasoning is a thinking process based on a rational method.

The concepts of reason, reasoning, historical reasoning have been applied by some philosophers who have made the historical study a distinct branch of history.

Presently the study of history has become a scientific inquiry into the problems of human past. The reflections on the historical inquiry have been taken up both by the historians and philosophers, more by the philosophers. This inquiry is based on reason. And the manner or process of these historical reflections may be called historical reasoning. The question of reason and historical reasonings are the issues of historical method, and so the main problem of the philosophy of history.

**Philosophy of history**

Study of history has come a long way since the time of Herodotus and Thucydides. The historians more or less deal with known aspects of human past. They deal with facts and interpretation of facts. Ranke in Germany and Auguste Comte in France gave great importance to facts and almost made the facts, the demigods of history. Philosophers normally do not deal with history or are not concerned much with philosophical reflections on history. However, Voltaire among the Enlightenment philosophers and Hegel among the Idealist thinkers had shown fresh thinking on history. It was Voltaire who, first used the term, "the philosophy of history which means a critical or scientific history, a type of historical thinking in which the historian made up his mind for himself instead of repeating whatever stories he found in old books" (R.G: Collingwood, Idea of History1946). Then Hegel in his *Lectures on the Philosophy of History*

(1822-23) meant by it a universal or world history. For Hegel, philosophy of history is not only a philosophical reflections on history but history itself raised to a higher power. He visualises a universal history of mankind. Hegel put history on the stage of the philosophical thought.

Auguste Comte and the Positivist school thought that philosophy of history was the discovery of general laws governing the cause of events which was history's business to reveal. The conceptions of Voltaire, Hegel and Comte are based on their respective philosophical concepts. To Voltaire, philosophy means independent and critical thinking; for Hegel, it is a thinking about the world as a whole. And for the Positivists, philosophy means the discovery of uniform laws.

In early 20th century, Croce in Italy propounded a philosophy of history that all history is contemporary history and that history consists essentially in seeing the past through the eyes of the present and in the light of its problem, And the main task. of the historian is not to record but to evaluate (E. H. Carr, *What is history?* p. 15, quoting B. Croce, *History as the story of Liberty,* 1941).

R.G. Collingwood, a profound philosopher of history regarded philosophy as a thought about thought. According to him, philosophy of history is the special enquiry into the special philosophical problem created by the existence of organised and systematized historical research" (Collingwood, p. 6). However, to E.H. Carr, the philosophy of history would mean the answers to the question "What is history" ?

**What is history?**

Therefore, the philosophy of history is concerned with all the basic issues of the hostorical method, starting with dermition, nature and objective ot history or historical knowledge, interpretation and the uses of history. History has been defined in different ways through the ages, starting from the humanistic Greco-Roman historiography (when history meant enquiry), Universalism of Medieval historiography, passing to the highly empirical liberal historiography of the nineteenth century, then to the highly critical and philosophic historiography of the twentieth century. However, in this paper, it is proposed to consider two views on the issue, a philosopher and an historian, R.G. Collingwood and E.H. Carr. Collingwood observes "All history is history of thought, and therefore all history is re-enactment in the historian's mind, of the thought whose history he is studying" (Collingwood, p. 215). History is a re-enactment of the past experience thought through the mind of the historian. Collingwood's view of history is more concerned with mode of reasoning Or the thinking of the historian on the past—it is more a philosophical enquiry of the past. This re-enactment or reconstruction of the past in the historian's mind is dependent on the empirical evidence. History is to be located in time and space, it is to be consistent with itself and based on evidence. His evidence necessitates that history has to deal with facts of the past which are re-enacted in the mind of the historian. The historian holds a key position in the whole process of enquiry and interpretation.

E. H. Carr thinks that "history is a continuous process of interaction between the historian and his facts, an unending dialogue between the present and the past". History is also a study of the causes of these facts of the past and interpreting them. Carr is perhaps not very far from Collingwood's idea in the interrelationship of the historian and facts (thought in the words of Collingwood), past and present through the thinking of the historian. But Collingwood is more abstract and philosophical while Carr is more empirical and interpretative. These two views of history have to be understood as they represent two trends in the historiography of modem times. They have raised study of history to a higher philosophic level.

In this context, history is now not only a true account of what really happened in the past, how and why of the past happenings. History means more an approach, a mode of enquiry to find the truth and interpret the truth to the relevance of the present. It has, therefore, become more a question of method. Hence, our concern with the Historical Method. How the historian re-enacts the past in his mind and how the historian conducts his interaction with his facts of historical evidence and how he carries on his dialogue between the past and the present, how the interpretation of the past facts is done, what is the role of reason or reasoning, historical thinking or reasoning, facts or historical evidence, these are the issues of the historical method.

**Reason in historical process and Historical reasoning**

Before we proceed to the analysis of the historical method, we have to examine the role of reason in history. While the empiricists do not give importance to this issue the Idealists particularly Hegel have strongly emphasised on the position of reason in the historical process. We have already explained the connotation of reason and reasoning which are the mental faculty behind the historical knowledge on historical thinking. Reason has been made a basis for historical process and historical reasoning. According to Hegel reason is the main spring of the historical process. What happens in history happens by the will of man as the historical process consists of human action and the will of man is nothing but man's thought expressed in action. Thus, it comes out of the mind and thought of man. Man is both rational and passionate. Both reason and passion are the deriving forces of the historical process. Hegel magnified the concept of the "cunning of reason" behind the growth of the universal history of mankind. "Reason whose plans are executed in history is neither abstract natural reason, nor transcendent divine reason but human reason and human passion". History is the reflection or manifestation of the self development or reason. Historical process is, at the bottom, a logical process. This position of Hegel leads him to think that history ends with the present and it has no future. Hegel's idea of history as a logical process developed in time has been opposed by thinkers like B. Croce for whom history is the story of human mind. J .B. Bury does not agree with Hegel's over emphasis on the rational elements in the historical process, because Hegel's system is marked by insufficient knowledge of facts and details.

Philosophy of history as A.C. Beard puts it, assumes the form of mvestigation on rational principles. And if history is a thought and a process of thinking, it is to be based on reason which is manifested in the historical knowledge. Then what is historical knowledge? According to Collingwood, "Historical knowledge is the knowledge of what mind has done in the past and at the same time redoing of the perpetuation of the past acts in the present." Here the historical knowledge (historical epistemology) is not mere accumulation of knowledge of the past but a continuing process of reasoning and examining the knowledge in the light of the present. For this conception, Collingwood has been criticized by E. H. Carr on the ground that it is giving too much of importance to the discretion of the historian which is dangerous for scientific truth. Naturally historical thinking or historical reasoning is a critical thinking, rethinking or reflecting for interpretation of the past thought and action of man as resorted to by the historian. While it is Marc Bloch who first uses the term "Historical Reasoning" in the *Historian s Craft* (1945), it is Collingwood who examines the question of historical thought and historical thinking. According to him, historical thinking or reasoning is an original and fundamental activity of the human mind dealing with the *Innate idea* meaning the idea of the past. Historical thought is an ever changing continuing phenomenon. It is "a river into which none steps twice".

The ultimate aim of historical thought of historical reasoning is to find out the historical truth which is a highly subjective propositions. We find here the importance of reasoning by historian in finding out the truth of the past facts and ultimately the historical truth which has relevance to the present.

To sum up, the philosophy of history has been concerned with the discovery of the past, meaning and interpretation of the historical phenomena, speculation about the nature and use of history and the investigation into the historical process. What will be the procedure of the historical thinking or reasoning has to be located in the method which has come popularly known as the historical method.

**The historical method**

The historical method has assumed a great importance with the development of scientific history. After a long debate; history has been put rightfully in the category of science, or to be precise, of social science. Science is both an accumulation of knowledge and a method of approach in the search of truth and knowledge. It is also a rational mode of analysis to arrive at and find out the truth. History, being a mode of rational enquiry, is science and real history is scientific history. And history adopts a scientific method which means a rational and logical mode of enquiry, analysis and generalisation. In short, the historical method is a tool to answer the questions of history like what happens, how it happens and why it happens. Historical method *is* essentially a scientific method, but the main difference between the two is in the use of data or evidence but the manner of inquiry, analysis, criticism, generalisation or interpretation is the same.

Historical method emerges out of the *necessity of looking* at events, institutions and ideas in the perspective of time as perceived by the present through the thinking process of those who study such historical phenomena. Historical method *is* the mode of historical reasoning adopted by the historian. Thus it covers the following postulates, phases and process.

(i) The location and selection of the historical facts, evidence of process relevant to the objective of the historical investigation.

(ii) Construction or reconstruction of the past based on the analysis of the facts and evidences.

(iii) Interpretation of the historical facts.

**Facts as historical evidence**

Primacy of facts in the historical study has been well established. Historical enquiry starts with the location and selection of facts which are essential for the construction of a phenomenon of history. All facts are not necessarily historical evidence, it is relative to objective, theme and manner of the historical evidence has been now called the source of history.

**Historical observation**

In the location and identification of facts, the mode of historical observation is applied. Here, the historical observation is different from the scientific observation which is carried out directly by the scientist who is working with a hypothesis. In case of historical observation, it is not possible for a historian to observe the happenings which constitute history. His observation is an indirect one, focusing on the facts or sources.

He is, of course, required to have a wide knowledge of human activities, past and present, which are related to the theme of his investigation. Peculiarity of historical observation is that it has to observe the events through documents, by reading or examination, which are evidences for a historical reconstruction.

**Authenticity of the evidence**

Once a fact has been located and identified as a historical evidence, the authenticity of the particular evidence is scrutinized, tested and finally proved. There are many instances in which books, chronicles, inscriptions and other historical evidences are forged. The crucial test of the reasoning faculty of the historian is on the establishment of the authenticity of the historical evidence. The principle of historical criticism, according to Marc Bloch, requires the asking of the questions as given below.

(i) Are the evidences forgeries or deceptive?

(ii) Do the evidences speak the truth?

(iii) How are the evidences to be subjected to scientific and rational scrutiny?

After the establishment of the authenticity of the evidences the historian, after his close observation and scrutiny, will assemble the documents which may be literary and archaeological. He can criticise, reject or accept the evidence based on his findings.

**Selection of evidences**

It is the prerogative or the discretion of the historian to select the evidences needed for his construction of the history of his field of study. But a practising historian following the historical method can not indulge in the irrational and irrelevant evidences. Otherwise his work will lack the rationality, consistency and relevance.

**Reconstruction of the past**

The facts, thus selected, will be subjected to historical analysis and utilized for the reconstruction of the past. In this process of historical analysis, the historical impartiality is to be rigorously applied for an objective judgement and understanding of the phenomenon of history. It calls for a rational organisation of the facts which Marc Bloch calls the raw materials of history. However different schools of historical writing have adopted different approaches in the construction of the past. For the determinist school of thought like the Marxians, the evidences of economic problem will be utilized for the writing of history based on economic determinism. This is greatly iinked up with the question of interpretation. Reconstruction and interpretation are dependent on the model of history writing which is adopted in a particular case. However, the historian's supreme duty is to explain the causes of the happenings in the past in this construction.

**Interpretation of the past**

The real testing of the historical method is on the question of interpretation which has been given so much of importance that historical method has been sometimes equated with the mode of historical interpretation. Whether, a history is a critical history or traditional history, or scissors and patch history (of Collingwood) or scientific history or deterministic history, it is dependent on the category of historical interpretation. The usual issues of the objectivity and generalization in history are engrained in this interpretation of the past.

**Historical objectivity**

Objectivity in history, in a negative sense, is not taking sides by the historian in the interpretation of history. He is both rational and passionate. Based on reason, a rational or objective history is expected from the historian. But subjectivity is an outcome of human passion and the historian also falls a prey to this subjective pressure. The colonial or imperial historiographer defends the imperial actions while the nationalist historian eulogises the patriotic acts and condemns the imperial authorities. A scientific historian is supposed to give an objective history. How the objectivity is to be established? For example, when a fact passes through the historian's mind the fact is coloured by his own prejudices, predilection and bias in his mind. The fact is already biased. When the fact is constructed into a historical canvass, the choice of the fact is not objective but subjective. Objectivity demands that when the fact passes through the historian's mind, his judgement should be free from prejudices and biases. While objectivity is definitely an ideal in the historical method, total objectivity can not be fully achieved. This is due to the very nature of history which is, as somebody said, not an exact science. We may refer to Ranke who is of the opinion that once the facts are subjected to criticism and cured of their dross by the historian's craftsmanship, the facts become pure and unalloyed historical gold. But human mind, so also the historian's is not that simple.

## Generalization

It was the Positivists who tried to locate the uniform laws out of the empirical historical data to explain the growth of the structure of society. They applied the principle of generalisation to find uniformity in the data to discover the universal laws. Positivist generalization is different from historical. generalization. After analysis of the historical facts, an abstraction is deduced to show certain common pattern or patterns in the historical development. This process of abstraction may be called generalization. As history is a social science, out of the historical data, a generalised pattern of history emerges through the abstraction.

## Periodization

History deals with time and space. So chronology and geography are important parts of a historical enquiry. But with the new philosophical approaches to history, the study of human history in terms of periods has been increasingly discarded and the study of specific problems of history (in the words of Acton) has become fashionable. Marx's economic interpretation of history has almost destroyed the chronological history. But so long, history continues to deal with the past of man, its concern with time and periodization will continue to exist in the historical method.

## REFERENCES

1. R.G. Collingwood, *The Idea of History.*
2. Marc Bloch, *The Historian's Craft.*
3. F. Braudel, *On History.*
4. E.H. Carr, *What is history ?*
5. N. Subramanim, *Historiography.*
6. J.B. Bury, *The Idea of Progress.*
7. Paul Edwards (ed.), *The Encyclopaedia of Philosophy, Vol. 7 and* 8.

CHAPTER THREE

# OBJECTIVITY IN THE HISTORIGRAPHY OF MANIPUR

## What is history?

This is a complex question. The attempt to answer this question has led to the emergence of historiography. The study of history has come a long way since the time of Herodotus and Thucydides. History has been defined in different ways and influenced by the ideas and intellectual ethos of a particular time. The rationalist Greco-Romans defined history as enquiry. History has become both a study of human society and mode of enquiry in which the historian occupies a prime position. History has become a historian's history, his creation, his perception and his interpretation. History is now not only what happened in the past, how and why of the past happenings; history means more an approach, a mode. of enquiry to find the truth and to interpret the truth to the relevance of the present. Therefore, history has become more a question of method.

## Historical method

Historical method is the mode of historical reasoning adopted by the historians. It emerges out of the necessity of looking at the historical phenomena in a scientific and rational perspective. After a long debate, history has now been rightly categorised as a science, a social science. Science is both an accumulation of knowledge and a method of approach in the search for knowledge and truth, a rational mode of analysis to arrive at truth. History, therefore, as a mode of rational enquiry is a science and its method is a scientific method. Historical method, in short, is a tool to answer the basic questions of history like what happens, how it happens and why it happens.

## Historical objectivity

Objectivity in the historical method is the rational and truthful interpretation of historical events. The real test of a historian is his objectivity. Objectivity will be achieved if the historian draws a purely rational, logical and impartial conclusion. His manner of drawing conclusion from the mass of evidences should be unbiased and free from prejudices. While objectivity is definitely an ideal in the historical method, it is difficult to achieve a total or pure objectivity. Human mind has both reason and passion. While objectivity is an outcome of reason, subjectivity is the reflection of his passion.

## Traditional Meitei historiography

Historiography is the art of writing history. The ancient Meiteis possessed a strong sense of history. The traditional concept of history is expressed by the Meitei word *Puwari* (story of forefathers). It is nearer to *Sanskrit Itihasa-Puran*, rather than English 'history' or Greek '*historia*'. The Meitei *Puwari* consists of legends, genealogy and historical accounts of their country. The creation myths or cosmological traditions, origin and genealogies of the clans, religious accounts, the dynastic accounts of the clan chieftains are given prominent place. Chronicles with or without chronology form the core historical literature. However, history as a separate academic discipline did not exist; it was a part of the whole gamut of knowledge. For example, a literary text of the 18th century, *Leithak Leikharon*, a compendium of myths, legends, genealogy, folklore, religious practice and social accounts, is not a history in the modern sense, but a standard book of knowledge which was expected to be possessed by a traditional Meitei scholar (Maichou). Chronicles are the backbone of the Meitei traditional historiography. The celebrated *Cheitharol Kumbaba* and *Ningthourol Lambuba* are the best examples. There was no separate discipline of history as such; history or historical knowledge was the part of the whole know ledge. Historical particularism did not exist outside the composite whole of human knowledge. Meitei world view was always holistic.

With the Sanskritization of Manipur, deliberate attempt was made by the Hindu scholars to imprint an Aryan and Hindu origin and identity on the Hindunised Meiteis, identification of religion and race had led to the emergence of a sense of distinct origin and a view of history in the ruling dynasty. History was given a sanskritized orientation which was reflected in the chronicles and genealogy of the ruling Ningthouja dynasty of Manipur. The keeping of chronicles which was an indigenous Meitei practice was given a chronological frame by the adoption of Hindu eras, for instance, the *Cheitharol Kumbaba* adopted three eras, *Kalyabda, Sakabda* and *Chandrabda*. *Ningthourel Lambuba* and other genealogical chronicles do not have chronology. This absence of time frame of chronology is a reflection of the Meitei concept of the past which was intermingled with the present. Past and present exist side by side in the Meitei psyche. The chronicles were not published but kept in the Royal college of Priests. As the *Cheitharol Kumbaba* was an official diary, the royalty's view and version of the events were recorded. An abridged edition of the Kumbaba was published first in 1939 by Thongam Madhob. The text of the chronicle was published in 1967, edited by L.M. Iboongohal Singh and N. Khelchandra Singh. The first history of Manipur, based on indigenous chronicles was *Manipur Itihas* written by Haodeijamba Cheitanya and was published in 1890. He was the first indigenous historian of Manipur, followed by Pukhrambam Parijat's *Manipur Purabrita* in 1917, Kaomacha's *Manipur Ittibritti* (1933), Mutum Jhulon's *Vijay Panchali* (1939), Atombabu Sharma's *Manipur Itihas* (1940). These works were influenced by Indian historiography. In the traditional Meitei historiography, religious ethos played a very important role: pre-Hindu Meitei religion, Vaishnavism and Aryanism.

### Colonial historiography

Colonial historiography in Manipur was started with R.B. Pemberton's Report on *North Eastern Frontier of British India*, 1835 which devoted a sizeable portion on Manipur's history, geography, economy and ethnography. Pemberton was the pioneer of modern historical studies. Pemberton's work was based on the style of James Mill's *History of India* (1819), the first history of India in English language. There were official reports published by the British officers posted as Political Agents in Manipur. Mention may be made of W. McCulloch's *Account of the Valley of Munnipore and Surrounding Tribes* (1859), R. Brown, *A Statistical Account of Manipur* (1874), E. W. Dun, *Gazetteer of Manipur* (1886, 1891). Jame Johnstone's My *Experience in Manipur and Naga Hills* (1895) which deal with a portion of history but history as such was not seriously attempted. The history of Manipur was first included by Alexander Mackenzie in his *History of the Relation of the Government with hill tribes of North Eastern Frontier of British Bengal* (1884) Mackenzie's History is an important contribution to the colonial historiography. Mackenzie as a chronicler and annalist had been quite successful, but as an analyst and critical historian much remains to be desired. Of the ethnographic work, T.C. Hodson's *The Meitheis* (1908) is an original research on the Meitheis of Manipur on anthropological and linguistic method. His work on the *Naga Tribes of Manipur* (1911), John Shakespeare's *Lushai Kuki Clans* (1913) are important sociological studies, but not history as such. Robert Reid's *History of Areas Bordering Assam* (1942) devotes a chapter on Manipur, a continuation of Mackenzie's work. These works give the colonial perspective on the history of the people of Manipur. But Robert Reid was neither a chronicler nor an analyst, he was a mere documentor. These colonial writings, scientific to some extent, are quite different from traditional Meitei writing on history. Abdul Ali's *Notes on Early History of Manipur* (1923) is an important work on the 18th century Manipur's relation with the British. Another aspect of colonial historiography was the beginning of archaeological studies: historical archaeology, epigraphy and numismatics.

Two divergent views of the parallel traditional historiography and the colonial historiography are reflected on the controversial Aryan origin of the Hinduised Meiteis. When the Hindu scholars struck to the sanskritized version of the Aryan origin of the Meiteis, the colonial ethnographers and historians refuted the theory and focused on the Mongoloid or Tibeto Burman roots of the people of Manipur, based on ethnography and linguistic. T. C. Hodson's magnum opus, *The Meitheis* which made the Meiteis known throughout anthropological world was not relished by the Meitei Hindu scholars, especially on the origin of the people. Pukhrambam Parijat's *Manipur Purabritta* (1917) and the writings of the great scholar, Panditraj Atombabu Sharma, especially *Haree Mayee,* Vedic interpretation of Manipur were attempts to establish the Aryan origin of the Meiteis. Hindu elite and members of the feudal nobility subscribed to this view. Therefore objectivity has been greatly blurred. A contribution of colonial historiography is that Manipur became widely known in English speaking India and Britain.

**Contemporary historiography**

During the post-second World War period, sporadic historical writings were published. R.K. Sanahal's *Manipur Itihas* (1947) is a land mark in history writing in Manipur. Though not trained in history professionally, R.K. Sanahal's profuse works are quite commendable. After independence, there was an attempt to look afresh at the past history. J. Roy's A History of Manipur (1958) was the first "real" history of Manipur dealing with the period since the 18th century. Despite some deficiency this work was widely circulated in India. However, credit should be given to R.K. Jhalajit Singh for his "A Short History of Manipur" (1965) which was based on indigenous sources, mostly hitherto unpublished royal chronicles, especially, Cheitharol Kumbaba and Ningthourol Lambuba. It was a history of the Ningthouja dynasty from the early period to the middle of twentieth century. His objective was to present a history of Manipur in the perspective of the growth of the Meitei kingdom and expansion of Aryan culture in Manipur. Deficiency in Roy's history has been greatly filled up by this history. Another landmark in the contemporary historiography was the publication of the royal chronicle, Cheitharol Kumbaba in 1967 by Manipuri Sahitya Parishad.

There was a great interval in historical studies in Manipur in 1970's. And during the next quarter of century, studies on history took a scientific form. The erstwhile Jawaharlal Nehru University Centre and now Manipur University have taken the lead in contemporary historical studies on Manipur. A large number of research works, mostly in the form of doctoral thesis were published on all periods of history, ancient, medieval and modem, both in English and Manipuri. Publication of the chronicles, historical texts and archival materials is a great aspect of Manipur's historical studies. Access to the sources of information had been provided by these publications. Archaeological studies, collection of inscription, coins and pre-historic excavation add to the development of pre-history of Manipur. Archaeological aspect of historical studies has been covered out now.

A very important trend in historical studies in Manipur is the reassessment or interpretation, in historical terminology, of history of Manipur by the new breed of academicians, historians, and social activists including come Young Turk intellectuals. The Sanamahi scholars have been harping on the pre-Hindu religions belief and focusing on the nonAryan indigenous identity of Manipur and her dominant people, the Meiteis. There was a stiff resistance from the great scho'ars of the Sanskritic School. But with the intervention of the anthropologists and linguists the Aryan origin of the Meiteis has been made an exploded myth. There was a fresh look at the British conquest of Manipur in 1891, full of passion and emotion, patriotic enthusiasm, scientific scrutiny and fresh interpretation. A huge literature grew up on the subject; Khongjom Parba has now become a popular history, with a continuing methodological controversy on the battle of Khongjom regarding the date of its happening. The colonial period has been thoroughly studied; anti colonial social protest movements, Kuki rebellion, Zeliangrong movement, Nupi Lal, etc. Another important reassessment has been raging in Manipur's academic and social circles on the role of the great revolutionary leader of Manipur, Hijam Irabot Singh, his ideology and thinking in shape offuture of Manipur and the controversial Merger Agreement of 1949 and concomitant issue of the political status of Manipur in the pre-Merger Period (1947-49).

These debates are expression of both academic interest

and ideology of the new breed of free thinking writers and activists. Here is the necessity of an objective and logical assessment of the real historical events. The attitude of 'I am the authority' reflected in academic debate should be discarded. Lastly, I am sure that the historical studies are in the right direction. Historians are not futurologists; but in the contemporary society of Manipur, history and students of history have been provided an opportunity and responsibility to tell the truth for the well being of the community. Research is in good progress in Manipur. Search for the truth and knowledge continues. I would like to remind the distinguished scholars of the duty of historians given by Goethe.

> " *The Historian s duty is to separate the truth from the false; the certain from the uncertain*"

**Periodization in the history of Manipur**

History as a study of society deals with time and space. Therefore, history cannot be divorced from the time- frame of the man's social development, hence, the continuing importance of "Periodization" in the study of history. At the same time, history is an unending river of events and there is no exactitude in the fixing of period in the historical canvass. The dividing line in history is more abstract than concrete. Historical scholarship or modern historiography is greatly influenced by the European historiography which is rooted in Greek and Roman historiography.

So study of history and historiography have become Euro-centric. Periodization can be categorised on the following three criteria:

(i) Time

(ii) Mode of production

(iii) Technology.

European history was periodized into three time frames: the Ancient, Medieval and Modern. Starting of the Modern

Age was the 16th century marked by the European Renaissance, Reformation, geographical discovery of different parts of the world and beginning of modern European colonialism followed by industrial and agrarian revolution. The period saw the culmination of the feudalism and development of capitalism along with European imperialism on non-European world. The ancient period was from the earliest time down to the 10th century. Coinciding with the growth of Greek civilization, Roman Empire and its decline and growth of Christianity and emergence of different kingdoms and principalities on the debris of Roman Empire. The Middle Age or the medieval period from the 11th to the 15th century marked by universalization of the Christian society, medieval religious obscurantism.

This periodization on the basis of time, namely, ancient, medieval and modem was the universal model. But with the growth of archaeology and anthropology as academic disciplines in the nineteenth century, the concept of "prehistory" on the basis of archaeological excavations and anthropological evidences of the non-European ancient societies has emerged. Now from "prehistory", archaeology has gone into all aspects of the historical theme in all periods of history. Without archaeological evidences, no history is now, complete.

Marx's economic interpretation of history - both as a tool of social science investigation and ideological plank for the communist revolution has revolutionised the study of history—on the basis of the role of the economic forces in shaping human society and civilization. He divides the progress of human social development into primitive communism, slavery based imperial system, the feudalism as a political system and mode of production and emergence of capitalism; and prophesied the socialist society and to communism. Periodization on time frame has been obliterated in Marxist political method—the mode of production from slavery to freedom of production. Periodization is also fixed on the basis of technology like the Palaeolithic (Old Stone) Age, Neolithic (New stone) Age, Chalcolithic (Copper and Bronze) Age, Iron Age, Steam Age, Nuclear Age, Space Age, etc.

However, the European and Indian system of periodization cannot be fitted into the scheme of periodization in the history of Manipur. Manipur is a cradle of civilization, her history was a historical evolution, independently developed in allong span of time. The problem arises out of the distinct sovereign status of Manipur; she was conquered by the British in 1891 and made a Native State from 1981 to 1947. Her separate political status made Manipur quite distinct from the other parts of British India.

Secondly, the fixation of the modem period in the history of non-European world of America, Africa, Asia and even Oceania, was made on their contact with the European powers, for example, the Battle of Plassey (1757) in India, the First Opium War (1839) in China, Perry's Expedition to Japan (1854) in Japan, the Treaty ofYandabu (1826) in Burma. If the European contact is the yardstick, in the case of Assam, the British conquest of Assam in 1826, was the beginning of modem period in Assam. So the modem age differs from one country to another in the non-European world. Within India also history of different states and region would have periodization different from the national historical periodization.

In the context of Manipur, the Indian "national" periodization scheme namely, Ancient, Medieval, Modem on the respective time frame, from the earliest to the 12th century A.D. from the 12th to the middle of 18th century and from the middle of 18th to the present does not suit to the scheme of historical time spanning. Suggestion has been made by some scholars on the following time - frame which is not suitable for Manipur.

(i) Ancient period: From the earliest time to the 12th century A.D.

(ii) Medieval period: From the 12th century A.D. to 1819, the beginning of the Seven Years' Devastation.

(iii) Modem period: From 1826 Treaty of Yandabu to the present.

This arrangement lacks justification both in the t ne-frame and theme of history. Some suggestions have been made for the consideration of the learned scholars.

**1. Ancient Period**

Manipur's Ancient Period may be traced from the earliest "prehistoric" time down to the completion of the formation of Manipur as a Sovereign state during the reign of King Kyamba who concluded external treaty with Kingdom of Pong (Shan State) of Upper Burma in 1471 A.D. (15th century A.D.) Manipur was evolved out of the integration of the clan regional principalities both political and social.

**2. Medieval period**

From the last quarter of the fifteenth century A.D. to the end of the nineteenth century, Manipur had risen to become an imperial power in the 17th and 18th centuries and began to decline till British conquest in 1891. Feudalism as a social, economic and political system was fully developed.

**3. Modern period**

Modem period may be fixed from 1891 A.D. when the British conquered Manipur: colonialism, feudalism and Indian administrative system were a fully operative during the period of the British Rule (1891-1947) Modern period continued after 1947. There is an opinion whether modem period should start form 1826 when Manipur was recognised an independent country by the Treaty of Yandabu. But Manipur did not lose her sovereignty despite the contact with British through the political agency.)

## 4. Contemporary history

Is a part or continuation of the modern period Post–Independence period from 1947 onwards is regarded as a contemporary historical period. Manipur is now a part of the Indian Republic and the national model of "contemporary period" as a sub-period has been adopted. Colonialism of the European type, feudalism and monarchy have been replaced by internal colonialism, democracy and capitalism.

Lastly, one wonders whether Manipur's association with India since 1947 and more particularly 1949, which is a part of modem period can be termed as a period of freedom, free from colonial shackles, under free India's democratic system or extension of the colonial rule in a different from.

## Activist interpretation of history

Historical scholarship has been confronted by an extraordinary state of activist interpretation of history. It is a part of the phenomenon of intellectual activism which has engulfed the socially conscious elite of Manipur, Historical study in Manipur has become a multidisciplinary study. Manipur's history has been examined from different angles by scholars of different non-history disciplines. This has added new dimensions to historical introspection. One of the consequences of this massive historical exercise is the emerging controversies on almost all landmark historical events, be that the Meitei conversion to Hinduism, the Kabaw valley issue, the Chronology of the Battle of Khongjom, the Merger Agreement of 1949 or even Rev. William Pettigrew's centenary celebration.

Ideology in terms of religious and political background, has been given a position of primacy. History, historical event and personality have been interpreted to suit the ideology of different social and political action groups with their ideologies or think tank having or propagating a particular historical viewpoint. The controversy on historical events and personalities is not doubt welcome as the quantum of critical analysis on them indicates their own importance and significance. The current debate on Merger of Manipur into India in 1949, the political status and the consequences of Merger, the perceived or imagined has gone beyond the parameter of historical enquiry. But historical interpretation of events cannot be abandoned by the historians to the activists alone. But truth or in historical terminology, facts must be stated and made known to the world. Truth can never be hidden for all time. It is a great challenge to the historians to speak the truth. I am happy that many historians have taken position on the current debate on contemporary historical event, which is a correct and objective interpretation. History is a useful and powerful tool of social and political change; this happened in Indian national liberation struggle, the Bolshevik and Chinese revolutions. Some time it can be a dangerous tool in the hands of Chauvinists and ultra nationalist regimes like Nazi rule under Hitler; his attitude towards the Jews, Europe and the world and how he was destroyed. Power-wielding elitist groups in a political system used or misused history for the achievement of their goals.

Manipur is passing through a phase of criss-cross of her history. Historical scholarship is facing a crisis of correct interpretation of historical events. There can be use and misuse of history. Therefore, I draw the attention of the learned scholars to this contemporary historical interpretation and reinterpretation. The rationality, objectivity, scientific temper and courage in telling the truth in the historians are called for now. This is an opportunity to test their sense of objectivity in historical interpretation in the face of certain inevitable social pressure. Historians should not be and cannot be neutral; they have to be objective and stand by the side of truth, whatever unpleasant it may be at times. Historical interpretation of the past in the light of the felt social needs of the present is at the root of the present spade of historical exercise.

CHAPTER FOUR

# SCIENTIFIC METHOD IN SOCIAL SCIENCE RESEARCH

## Social science research

Social science research is a systematic method of exploring, analysing and conceptualizing social life in order to extend, correct or verify knowledge about it. Social science is concerned with the discovery and interpretation of social process, pattern of social behaviour and their similarities and dissimilarities which apply to typical social phenomenon.

## Scientific method

Research is the quest for knowledge and truth. Research methodology is the mode of enquiry which includes all aspects of research - starting from the identification and formulation of problem of research and its objectives, the technology of collecting data, interpretation of the data and analysis of the findings of the investigation.

Science is both an accumulation of knowledge and a method of approach in the search for truth and knowledge. It is also rational mode of analysis to arrive at or find out the truth. Therefore, scientific method in research naturally means a rational and logical mode of enquiry, analysis and generalization of a problem of investigation. It implies the following as given by Prof. B.K. Roy Burman.

(i) A precise formulation of the problem to be investigated.

(ii) Formulation of a working or explanatory hypothesis.

(iii) Observation and exploration of the problem of a variety of scientific techniques.

(iv) Uniform recording of the data obtained.

(v) Classification of the data

(vi) Interpretation or scientific generalization of the data.

A scientific method aims both at the analysis and abstraction of the data into an acceptable theory as one of the conclusions, prediction of particular behaviour in a given circumstance and scientific explanation of a social phenomenon. Therefore, a scientific method includes concept, hypothesis, conceptualization and theory. Concepts are the ways of perceiving a phenomenon; hypothesis is a presumed proposition formulated for empirical testing; conceptualization is the process of generalization of the data. And a theory is an integral body of definition. Assumption and general proposition covering a given subject matter from which a comprehensive and specific principles are deduced logically. A theory may be regarded as a tool of science and a sum total or product of a scientific investigation. Social science research is expected to build up theories and laws to explain the social phenomenon and mode of social enquiry. Theory defines the major orientation of a science. It is a conceptual scheme for systematization, classification and inter-relation of the relevant social phenomenon. It is also a system of generalisation of empirical facts. A theory can predict facts and points to the gaps in our existing knowledge.

## Identification of formulation of a research problem

A researcher is expected to gather as much knowledge as possible about his theme before he starts the research investigation. His awareness of the problem and orientation to it will enable him to identify the area, theme and relevance of his research problem. A rapid survey has to be made on the works done on the subject by others. It is called an appraisal of the historical situation. This is the study of the existing literatures and data on the problems. Then one has to find out the gaps in the research on the subject. In identifying a problem, a researcher has to find out the relevance, viability or feasibility and the original contribution to knowledge and availability of the data on the proposed study. One can formulate hypothesis, if any, to be tested in the study. The objectives of the research problem have to be examined and explained convincingly. It is to be clear whether the nature of the proposed study would be descriptive, analytical and just a reassessment of the subject.

**Collection of data**

Data is the crucial factor in a social science research; viability, authenticity and generation of data would decide the fate, success or failure of any investigation. The usual technique of the collection of the data includes:

(i) The examination of the documentary or literary sources, published and unpublished, primary and secondary. Such sources may include archive records in case of historical data, census reports, national sample survey and other offi cial documents.

(ii) Survey research

(iii) Observation which includes (a) non-controlled non-participant observation, (b) non-controlled participant observa tion, and (c) controlled observation.

(iv) Interview

(v) Direct management

(vi) Projection

Collection of data will differ in its manner according to the mode of collection of data, for example, the collection of literary sources, collection of information in the fields by means of canvassing of schedules, questionnaire and interview. Care should be taken in the selection of respondents in this type of data collection where sampling is adopted. There are different types of sampling in the selection of the respondents: random sampling, systematic sampling, stratified sampling, cluster sampling and multi stage sampling etc.

While the data is enormous, the researcher faces the problem of rejecting a data and accepting another one. In such situation, the principle of selection is to be adopted according to the need and requirement of the research. At the same time, one has to test the authenticity of data (especially of the oral evidences) by cross checking and collaborating with other existing data.

**Interpretation and analysis of the data.**

All the data need not be coded. But the data from the well prepared questionnaire and schedules are to be coded to get a systematic tabulation of the needed information. Data, after being coded is interpreted. The interpretation of the data depends on the need and nature of the problem. Data based analysis should be carefully handled with the intellectual acumen, sense of objectivity and power of generalization and abstraction of the empirical data. Empiricism and abstractionism are to be combined and harmonized.

**Presentation of the finding of the research Activities of the Institution**

After having accumulated the facts and analysed them, the researcher has to present his findings. It involves, of course, the description of the facts and analysis of the facts. Facts do not organise themselves into concepts and theories except within the conceptual framework. Unorganised facts will be just chaos. Contingent fact of historical research is to be kept in mind. It is the real test of the intellectual power of the investigator in this most important aspect of research work. It is commonly believed and said that, the analysis of the facts is to be rational, critical and logical to make it an objective assessment. The scientific temper of the researcher is the key to the success of the scientific method of investigation in any field. It is possible to adopt different models of analysis ranging from the doctrinaire Marxian, to historical, sociological or loosely worded scientific methods. Emphasis has been given by many social scientists, that in the presentation of his findings, the usual technique of writing, like foot notes, subheadings, chapterization, charts, maps and graphs are to be properly and faithfully followed.

The format of presentation or in common parlace, chapterization should cover the following aspects:

(i) Introduction covering the statement of the problem of the study, the objective and scope of the study, sources of information, critical review of the existing literatures and previous research, if any, concepts and theoritical forma tion and the justification of the study - a brief note on the research design including the universe, samples and sampling design techniques of data collection and data processes.

(ii) The major findings of the study giving the highlights of the major findings.

(iii) Discussion of the major conclusions arrived at including the interpretation of the study.

(iv) Summary and conclusion

(v) Bibliography and appendices

This format may be stretched according to the nature of the subject of research.

**Two problems of methodology in social science research.**

There are two popularly talked about methods in·social

science research: (i) Inter-disciplinary Research and (ii) Statistical Method, the question of inter-disciplinary research and the adoption of statistical method. It is true that every problem is multi-dimensional in nature.

Therefore, it can be better solved by multi pronged attacks. Hence the inter-disciplinary research is the need of the contemporary research an all branches of knowledge including social science.

(i) Inter-disciplinary research means an integrated approach in the enquiry into a research problem by using different tools and techniques of different disciplines.

(ii) It involves the engagement of scholars of different disci plines in tackling different aspects of the multi-dimensional problem.

(iii) It calls for a detailed and comprehensive statement of prob lems and identification of the units of the study in which the diverse disciplines with different tools may be involved.

(iv) It is also needed to harmonize the different tools of research and calls for a perfect co-ordination at the operational level.

(v) If these conditions are fulfilled, a comprehensive conclu sion can be drawn out of the investigation. And the interdisciplinary research will be successful.

**Adoption of statistical method.**

Everybody has been adopting the statistical method in social science research, especially, in economics, political science, psychology, education, sociology, anthropology and commerce. However, it is found that the quantification method which is a part of the statistical method can not be easily applied to history, though it has been adopted in economic and demographic history. Statistical method is to be sharpened in tackling issues of social science research.

In conclusion, it is to be stated that in social science research, not a single technique or not a single method is exclusively applicable to each and every problem. No method is fully proof system. Therefore, the social scientists apply different methods or techniques and tools to suit their specified areas and themes. The above techniques are, therefore, tentative.

## CHAPTER FIVE

# ETHNO-HISTORY

**Ethnos and ethno-history :**

Ethnos in Greek, means people. The Soviet sociologists have developed theoretical generalization on the concept of ethnos. Yulian Bromley describes ethnos as the bearer of relatively stable common features of culture including language. Thus, ethnos is a specific human entity, tribe, peasant community, nationality or nation even. An ethnos should have certain specific cultural features as its basic attributes, like common origin, language, social system, and religious beliefs, with a definite territory. In simple words, it is an ethnic group, an ethno cultural entity. And ethno-history means the history of an ethnos or the ethnic group. However, historically speaking, according to Bernard S. Cohn, ethno-history was originally adopted to describe the writings and research on the history of the indigenous peoples of the new world. It was a method developed by the American anthropologists to study the history, culture, society and identity formation of the American Indian tribes. It was John Reed Swanton, an anthropologist who developed and employed the ethno historical method in his *"The Early History of Creek Indians and their neighbourhood* (1922), *Primitive American History* (1940) and *The Indians of south eastern United States"* (1940).

Since then both historians and social anthropologist have extensively adopted the ethno-historical method in anthropological and historical studies. Gradually in the West, ethno-history has come to mean any historical study of non-European people or history of indigenous people before and after European contact, utilizing documents, oral and anthropological evidences and adopting the conceptual framework of cultural and social anthropology.

**Ethno-historical Method:**

Starting as an essentially anthropological tool adopted by the anthropologists using historical evidences, ethnohistory has been further developed into a dual disciplinary method, combination of historical sources and ethnohistorical field work. This method is utilized to bring out, in the words of Bernard Cohn, "a rounded history of the social and cultural system of any indigenous people, tribal groups, literate or illiterate of any ethnic group in any country". Ethno-history has assumed a greater significance with the ever increasing feeling of ethnicity of almost every social group, specially the minorities in different parts of the world. Ethnicity has been defined by Clifford Geertz as the 'primodial consciousness[1], of a social group namely, the feeling of the original beginning. With the emergence of ethnicity, ethnohistory has been called upon to examine the ethnic processes of the concerned groups. The method or approach of the ethno-historical study is concerned with the nature of the society, period, type, demarcation of the habitat and kinds of documentation available and theoretical formulations.

**History and ethno-history**

Attempts have been made to differentiate the conventional history and ethno history, though the barriers between the two are breaking down, as historians have started using anthropological and sociological tools in historical study. Both history and ethnohistory (which has common attributes of history and social anthropology) have used almost similar sources of information, written documentary sources, oral tradition and evidences and archeological sources. Yet one finds certain difference in emphasis. For example, the ethno-historian thinks in systematic functional terms, rather than in terms of accidents or particulars; the ethno-historian tries to perceive historical events from the point of the ethnoses or the people concerned, impact of the colonial policy or the policy of the rulers on their social, cultural and economic life. At the same time, one finds the similarity in the role of the conventional historian and the ethno-historian if we emphasise the role of the historian as a chronicler of events and an analyst of the historical development in a conceptual generalisation.

## Scope of ethno-history

Any ethno-historical study will cover the following aspects concerning the particular ethnic group or social entity to be studied.

(i) Geographical habitat and its ecology and environment

(ii) History of migration

(iii) Identity

(iv) Cultural adaptation to envircnments

(v) Demographic history

(vi) Relation of the group towards the colonial powers in tenns of trade, commerce, cultural contacts and political relation.

(vii) Ethnic process and ethnic identity expansion process

(viii) Endogenous and exogenous changes in the society due contact with the colonial rulers.

(ix) Ethnohistorical study should be diachronic dealing with a given pe riod; so it covers prehistory, historical period including pre colonial and post colonial period

Ethno-history is essentially concerned with the preliterate or non literate and post literate stage of the particular social group but it extends over all periods of history.

**Sources of ethno-history**

Sources will naturally include written documents, official records which cover the colonial period or the post colonial period, the oral traditions dealing with the origin, migration, settlement history, rites, rituals, social customs etc. Hence, information are to be collected from intensive field work with anthropological tools and techniques. The archaeological evidences are important sources like the prehistoric tools, the Palaeolithic and neolithic tools and implements. Now these facts or evidences have to be utilized to portray the history, society, culture, polity and economy of the group.

**Ethno-history of Manipur : its prospects**

Manipur's history is so far concerned with the evolution of the Meitei polity, society and culture in the valley of Manipur. This valley based history is due to the abundance and availability of the sources on Meitei history, whereas the surrounding hill tribes do not have the written records of their past. However, historical records are available since the colonial period. The vast and rich literature of the Meiteis, dealing with the religious, secular or creative, and historical subjects provide the source materials for the reconstruction of the history of the kingdom of Manipur. However, one finds the ethno-historical trends in the historiography of Manipur; T.C. Hodson's magnificent work, *The Meitheis,* gives the ethnographic, cultural and linguistic background to the history and society of the Meiteis. It greatly reinforces the study on the history of Manipur.

For writing the history of the hill tribes who are divided into two major ethnic groups: the Nagas and the Kukis, the ethno-historical method has been found to be the most effective one.

There are several areas of research where the ethno-historical method can be applied.

(1) The ethnic process of the evolution of the Meitei society covering the social and polity fonnations

(2) Evolution of the Meitei religious rite, rituals and festivals

(3) Migration of the hill tribes

(4) The cultural adaptation of the various tribal groups in the ecological setting of Manipur

(5) Inter-tribal and tribal and non-tribal contacts in terms of trade, commerce, cultural and administrative activities

(6) Ethnic processes among the hill tribes; identity expansion movements and other social movements which require extensive utilisation of oral evidence and tradition

**Some studies on the ethno-history of Manipur**

There are a few works dealing with ethnic groups of Manipur based on the ethno-historical method. Most of the works on the hill tribes are purely anthropological. But they may also be covered by ethno-history. Important works on tribes of Manipur like T.C. Hodson '*The Naga Tribes of Manipur(1911)*. John Shakespeare's *Lushai Kuki Clans* (1912), William Shaw's *Thadou Kukis* (1930), M. Horam's *Social and Cultural Life of the Nagas : The Tangkhuls*, H. Kamkhenthang's *Paite : A Transborder Tribe of India and Burma* are sociological and anthropological studies. T.C. Hodson's The Meitheis (1908) is a classic example of both anthropological and ethno-historical study. Gangmumei Kabui's Anal: A Trans border Tribes of Manipur and *The Koirengs of Manipur;* and Josheph Athickal's *The Marams: A Socio-Cultural Study* are ethnohistory.

## Limitations of ethno-history

One should be cautioned that ethno-history has certain limitations. It tends to be too much anthropological biased and loses the perspective of ethno-history. Therefore, one should be extremely careful in making a balanced approach to the study of this nature. But dealing with the history of the tribes in India, one cannot but apply the ethno-historical method.

In writing the history of the tribes of Manipur, we have to use ethnographic data over and above the usual historical data to arrive at a rounded or comprehensive history. The ethno-historical approach tends to be insular but the national, regional or sub-regional perspective should not be ignored. However, despite limitations, this approach is a workable method.

## REFERENCES

1. Yulian Bromley, *Ethnography,* 1973, Moscow quoted in Victor Kozlov in Ethnos and Culture in Ethno Cultural Development of African Countries, Moscow, 1984, pp. 25-29.
2. Bernard S. Cohn, in *International Encyclopaedia of Social Sciences on Ethno-History.*
3. Journals like, *Ethnohistory* (1954), Journal of American History are devoted to ethnohistory, both theoretical and empirical issues.

## CHAPTER SIX

# PARTICIPATORY RESEARCH

This is an account of an intellectual partnership between an anthropologist and historian through participatory research or action research.

### Intellectual Adventure

Sometimes in 1962, somebody told me that an eminent anthropologist named Dr. B.K. Roy Burman wanted somebody to accompany him in a field trip to a tribal village at the outskirts of Imphal. Fresh from the University in my early twenties, I was very keen to meet the anthropologist and visit the village. Then I met Dr. B.K. Roy Burman and we visited the village, a few miles from Imphal. I acted as an interpreter. I was very much impressed by his dexterity and skill in keeping the tribal peasants at case, putting questions in an easy style and getting the desired information, and also by his love for the poor tribal and commitment to the understanding of the tribal mind which is so simple and yet so elusive, I was interested in Dr. Roy Burman, because, he was an anthropologist and I have always loved social anthropological writings, though I am not a student of anthropology. I never imagined that this chance encounter in that afternoon would have started an intimate friendship and a close association which has lasted for the last thirty five years. For the next ten years, our association was occasional. He had sent me his occasional papers on tribal problems and publications of the Census of India. I received Worumung, a classic study of an year Ao Naga village as a new present, also the festivals of Manipur. Other village monographs made one interested in the micro level study of a society from the village level.

Mostly through the introduction of Dr. Roy Burman, I came to be associated with the academic exercises of the leading social scientists of the country on the problem of the north-eastern India under the auspices of the Department of Sociology of Delhi School of Economics, the Indian Council of Social Science Research and the Anthropological Survey of India. When I was in the Jawaharlal Nehru University, Post Graduate Centre in 1972, Dr. Roy Burman presented me his book on Demographic profiles of the Hill areas of North East India, which is still one of the best introductions to the land and people of north-eastern India. Dr. Roy Burman's understanding of the issues, ethnic, economic, cultural, linguistic and political, are lucidly presented in this book despite the fact that it is an official publication. I started to understand Dr. Roy Burman and to share his conviction that the problem of north-east India had a national importance because the basic ideals of the Indian nation are being put on trial by the ethnic minority problem of the sensitive region. Even when he was holding an official position, he did not remain confined to the narrow and rigid boundary or parameter of an official demographer. He has all the time been writing more as a social scientist trying to inform the nation about north-east and making the people of north-east feel that the nation understands their problems. His treatment is unorthodox and fresh. He also speaks of the geo-political significance of north-east India, because of its location at the tri-junction of south, south-east and east Asia. It is, in his works a spatial crucible, where national scholars are called upon to carry on experiments in living in peace and amity for ensuring the quality of life of their population.

In the mid-seventies, I was unwittingly engaged in a number of the studies: an ICSSR sponsored study of the educational problems of scheduled castes and scheduled tribes, and the socio-economic life of the Anal tribe and ethnographic account of the Koireng tribe of Manipur. By coincidence Dr. B.K. Roy Burman was awarded the prestigious Jawaharlal Nehru Fellowship at this time and he joined the Jawaharlal Nehru University as an Honorary Professor. Prof. Roy Burman was making an examination of the factors and processes of ethnic boundary maintenance and changes and the contribution of socio-economic and political development to the same. I took advantage of his presence in making my study from the stage of preparation and canvassing of schedules, to that of the collection of information through discussions in groups or with individuals. He was kind enough to be involved in my study and I in his study. There was convergence of interests of both of us.

Our joint academic venture may be divided into three phases: the first phase relates to our intensive enquiry at the field level among the tribes of Tengnoupal District, namely, Moyon of Komlathabi, Monsang of Liwachaning, Purum or Chothe of Purumchumbang, Taraos of Leishokching, Anal of Chandel and Chakpikarong; the second phase concerns the preparation of a *Forest Atlas of Manipur* by the joint efforts of a number of scholars, belonging to the field of cartography, history, anthropology and economics. They were mostly associated with the Post Graduate centre of Jawaharlal Nehru University at Imphal. Some were also working in various colleges of Manipur. In this phase we collaborated in organising seminars on different aspect of the problems of development. It was a preparatory work for a national workshop on social factors of development in Manipur which was sponsored by the Jawaharlal Nehru University with the active support from the Government of Manipur. It was to be inaugurated by Mr. P.N. Haksar, the then Deputy Chairman of Planning Commission. It was a multidisciplinary academic exercise with participation of different sections of the academic and non-academic community. The pre-workshop seminars provided the background of the problem of development in different regions of the state. It is unfortunate that the workshop could not take place for reasons beyond the control of the organisers including myself and Professor Roy Burman. However, during this period of intensive and extensive academic works, a national symposium on tribal demography was held in 1976 at Imphal which was attended by a large number of leading social scientists of the country including anthropologists, demographers, economists, geographers and administrators. Prof. Roy Burman was the Director of the National Symposium. Preparatory to this symposium a large number of write-ups on the ethnography of almost all communities were prepared by a group of young scholars and were published in the series called **'The Indigenous people of Manipur'** in the weekly **'Resistance'**. A great intellectual climate was generated in this part of the country.

**Method of Participator Resound**

The third phase, which is a continuous one is concerned with the building up of an organisational structure for participatory research on issues connected with tribal development and related matters. This was concreitised when the Institute of People's Action was established at Awangkhul in early 1977. The three phases of academic exercise are the reflection of the process of participatory learning, communication and action in social science. The basic issue in this process of academic and intellectual exercise is the question of "participation" of the researchers and the members of the group or of the community who are also the subjects and not more objects of such an academic enquiry. The process of participatory learning and communication is basically the process of collaborative identification of the relevant issues, their examination in depth through a series of group discussions and discussions with key informants, formulation of tentative answers and mobilisation of the requisite efforts at various levels for operationalising the same. It involves collection of information, documentation, analysis and understanding of the problem by the social scientists and the people acting together and interacting with one another. Thus, persons who belong to the different categories and levels of education, social and economic background including academics and administrators the village elders, and the village youth including women, and the common people share experiences and endeavours. The modality and form of participatory communication are group discussion, seminar, symposia, *workshop* as well as person to person exchange of information and ideas in problem identification and problem Solving situations. The purpose of these public discussions is to inform and to be informed or to educate and to be educated on specific issues, to collectively analyse and draw conclusions or prescribe remedies or solutions. The underlying assumption is that through intensive interaction of the scholars and the community, by simultaneously taking the roles of learner and educator; the various aspects of the situation comes out on the surface in a realistic manner and the intellectual moral basis for mobilisation is created. Participatory action is a more evolved form of action gone through by the social scientists with the participation of the people of different categories; the findings of such investigations are also continuously monitored.

During the time of the research investigation, it was found that ethnographic information of limited validity was available only about some of the tribes of Manipur. The colonial administrators like T.C. Hodson *(The Naga Tribes of Manipur*, 1911), John Shakespeare *(Lushai Kuki Clans*, 1913), William Shaws *(Notes on Thadou Kukis*, 1932) had of course written in considerable detail about many tribes of Manipur, form their point of view. These are also several post-Independence publications like RochungaPudaite's *Education of the Hmar People* (1960), Horam's Naga Polity K. B. Singh's (ed) *An Introduction to Tribal Culture and Language of Manipur*. Several educated tribal persons, even without social science background also started writing about the tribal communities. Professor R ›y Burman acted as the kingpin in the research investigation on the tribes of Manipur. He surrounded himself with a number of scholars belonging to different disciplines and it was decided to formulate a strategy of research in an unorthodox manner. On examination of the available ethnographic data, issues for confirmation of the existing data of hypothesis for collection of supplementary information new sets of data and for interpretation of the same were drawn up and discussed with selected persons of the tribal communities was well as other interested scholars. We chose Chandel district for our study. I was already engaged in the study of Anal tribe of the district. Apart from the enquiry into the socio-econimic changes in the Anal Society. The concepts of bridge-buffer communities as formulated by Prof. Roy Burman were found to serve as useful tools of analysis. The issue of identity was also linked up with the relation of the Anals with the kindred tribes, like Moyon, Monsang, and Lamkang. So within Chandel district, we selected Komlathabi, the most important village of the Moyons as the starting point of our investigation. We also studied the Monsang village of Liwachaning, Purumchumbang, the village of the Purums, now called Chothe, who have been made internationally famous by the earlier writings of T.C. Das. The other Purum village, Purum Pantha and Purum Lainingkhul were also studied by us. The studies at Komlathabi and Liwanchaning indicated the trends of changes in the identity equation of the Moyon and Monshang tribes who at one stage agreed to be known by a common name Mon. However, the Monsang youth of Liwachaning were opposed to this 'Mon' concept and wanted to keep to their Monsang identity.

**The Komlathabi model**

A symposium under the direction of Prof. Roy Burman was organised at Komlathabi to discuss the problem of development in Tengnoupal (now Chandel) district. A large number of persons, the village chiefs among whom mention should be made of Late R. Thoma, chief of Komlathabi, the members of the District Council, school teachers, government officers and students of the district participated in the symposium. The issues discussed at Kornlathabi were reported by a prestigious national journal **The Economic and Political Weekly** which was commented on by Ashok Mitra, an eminent administrator, scholar and demographer in the Presidential address of the symposium on Tribal Demography held in 1976. He said, "the proceedings of the symposium organised at Komhithabi throw a flood of light in this moulding process (of modernization) that is under way. They also give us an idea of the large number of tribal elite and non-elite who were aware of the deleterious as well as beneficial aspects of this moulding process" Quoting R. Thoma, the 70 years old doyen of the chiefs of the area, Ashok Mitra identified four spots which mark the most important aspects of the tribal way of life today. They are (a) The problem of forest utilization, (b) the problem of shifting cultivation and the proposed law of granting pattas, (c) the erosion of village authority and (d) the role of financial institutions. The Kornlathabi symposium was the precursor of a series of discussions. At that time the Tengnoupal Autonomous District Council appointed a Customary Laws Codification Advisory Committee with Prof. Roy Burman as Chairman, the Deputy Commissioner of Chandel, the

Chairman of the AutonomouS District Council and myself as members. The interactions with the villagers who were regarded as knowledgeable on their customs was very effective in understanding the structure and process of changes in tribal societies in Tengnoupal district. The tribal were very concerned with the status of chieftain-ship in different tribes; their mode of selection particularly whether it was based on hereditary or elective principle or on popular oligarchic selection subject to popular confirmation was found to have practical implication in interpreting the land holding system.

The spirit of Komlathabi caught up everybody including the distinguished participants of t .e symposium on tribal demography. A field session of the symposium was held at Saikot, a Hmar village in Churachandpur district. A paper on Saikot village prepared locally was discussed in the village itself. It was a unique experience for most of the participants in the symposium.

As a follow up action of the Komlathabi symposium and other seminars, a study entitled Operation Storm (Study own resources and Manpower) was undertaken in 33 villages with the voluntary assistance of the youth of the village. But the universal bench mark survey undertaken by the Department of Economics and Statistics, Government of Manipur for the preparation of tribal sub-plan reduced the motivation and felt need for STORM. 'In any case the voluntary participation of the village youth in such a survey based on a well throughout village schedule was in interesting experience for the people of the area as well as for the researchers. Perhaps this was one of the earliest experiments in participatory research in the country-much before the word became fashionable in social science organ.

The seminars which were organised at the district level, while making preparations for the proposed workshop in the social factors of development were held at Ukhrul, Kakching and Tamenglong more or less on the lines of the Komlathabi symposium. The problems of socio-economic development were discussed among the villagers, scholars and administrators of the district. While, every seminar reflected the peculiar problems of the district the basic issue remained the same as those of the Komlathabi symposium.

**The Institute of People's Action (IPA), Awangkhul**

The villagers of Awangkhul, a Rongmei village in Tamenglong district had been making contact with me for establishment of an institution which would bring development of this village community. Originally, it was proposed to set up a centre which would be a meeting place of the thinking minds of the country. I mentioned this to Prof. Roy Burman during a trip from Imphal to Silchar in December 1975. I requested him to visit Awangkhul and discuss the matter with the villagers. Prof. Roy Burman and myself visited Awangkhul in 6th December 1976. The villagers requested Prof. Roy Burman again to establish one action research institute and donated 200 acres of land for the purpose. Prof. Roy Burman who was associated with the Jawaharlal Nehru University as a Honorary Professor requested Dr. B. V. Ranga Rao, Chairman, Centre for Studies in Science Policy of J.N. U. to depute some scholars to Awangkhul to make a systematic study of its development potential. Dr. Rao deputed Shri V. R. Gammadi, M.Sc. (Chemistry) and Shri E.V. Ranga Mohan, B.Tech. (Hon). Agriculture to undertake a survey of land and forest resources, productive activities and living, conditions of the people of Awangkhul. They stayed in the village for three weeks during January-February, 1977 and prepared a useful report. It was presented to a general meeting of the villagers, which discussed it item by item for several hours on 7th February, 1977 and with certain modifications approved the same for operationalising through their collective efforts. The same day a formal resolution was adopted to establish the Institute of People's Action (IPA) which is a registered body.

**IPA**—Experiment of Community Land Based Development Awangkhul covers an area of about 200 sq. km. (20 km x 10 km) with a population of 540 persons in 96 households. Awangkhul means in Meitei language, a village on lofty height. But with the beginning of the construction of New Cachar Road (Now a national Highway connecting Imphal and Silchal), in 1968, the new settlement was established on the roadside hy some enterprising villagers. The land was plenty and development was envisaged hy utilizing the land natural resources of the village.

It is not the intention of the author to enumerate the activities of the IPA during the past ten years of its existence. But some idea of the nature of its activities will be given here. The IPA had adopted certain basic measures for the development of the village in agriculture and forestry, for providing the infrastructure for educational and social welfare; for child care, artistic and cultural development of the villagers. The IPA's structure of decision making is a composite one, consisting of the Board of Trustees, the traditional village council and the village community as a whole. Apart from Prof. Roy Burman as chairman the Board of Trustees includes the septuagenarian humanist P.B. Singh, who was once chief minister of Manipur and after abhorring politics has been working for broad based inter-ethnic amity and understanding in this part of the country where insurgency and violence have become an endemic feature for about two decades. Other members are Sanamani Yambem, a young scholar, myself and representatives of the village council. In acutal pratice, no important decision of IPA is taken without threadbare disucssions, lasting over hours involving the entire adult population of the village. Here is to be noted that for reclamation of the land of IPA, the entire adult population of the village rendered three days free labour every month for four years. The target is to generate enough income of the farm of IPA so that education, health-care and other essential needs of the villagers can be met out of the same.

The philosophy of IPA is informed management of the resources, self-reliance and community "participation in the formulation and implementation" and share of benefits of "development" as envisaged by the state bureaucracy. But at the same time according to the need of the situation IPA has involved itself in development activities as well. The IPA constructed a community cum guest house, a Jawahar Bal Bhawan, a centre for tribal performing arts, rural marketing centre for cane and bamboo works and a weaving centre. A remarkable achievement of the Institute which brought about tremendous change in the life of the village was the survey and distribution of traceable land to all families of the village. The JNU report mentioned earlier, highlighted on poverty of the village. On the initiative of the IPA, the **Nungba Integrated Hill Area Development Project** extended financial assistance for the construction of terraces by the villagers. With the reclamation of wet lands for cultivation on the banks of the Ijeti river, the people of Awangkhul who are basically shifting cultivators and were at that time more familiar with the use of hoe, have learnt the arts of ploughing by bullock and the ancillary practices in their fields. The IPA carried out adult education programme in thirty villages in the district in 1978-79. The IPA took great interest in the educational development of the villagers. It lent the services of its organiser as the headmaster of the local school for two years free of honorarium. IPA started a social forestry programme for the first time in western Manipur in 1979. A survey of crafts practised at Awangkhul and the adjoining village was conducted and on the basis of this survey report, one Rural Marketing Centre for cane and bamboo works was established with the assistance received from the All India Handicraft Board through Bharatiya Adimjati Sevak Sangha, Delhi.

IPA devoted its attention to the development of women and child welfare as well. Two creches were established at Awangkhul; four more were established in the neighbouring villages. In 1983, Tamenglong district was affected by severe food scarcity. IPA organised famine relief measures. Besides, on its initiative a consumer cooperative society has been established at Awangkhul which distributes consumer goods to the villagers. The IPA had also organised a primary school for the village children. But as tne Government has moved in to establish one school of its own, it was found difficult to continue the school started by IPA. At the same tine, the need of educational institution suitable to the socio-cultural and techno-economic milieu continues. After requisite preparation, both the pedagogical and ideational nature, IPA proposes to resume its activity in this matter.

With the assistance obtained from Jawaharlal Nehru Memorial Fund, a Jawahar Bal Bhawan was also established by IPA in 1979. On 12th April 1981 Smt. Indira Gandhi, late Prime Minister of India, visited Awangkhul and inaugurated the Bal Bhawan building. One of the important activities ancillary to the establishment of the Bal Bhawan is the development of a centre of tribal performing arts. A cultural troupe formed Primary based on the infrastructural and instructional facilities provided from here, has gone round the country. It gave a performance at Delhi on the occasion of the visit of the Vice-President of Mongolian Republic to India. A tribal and folk art festival was also organised in May 1982 with the assistance provided by Sangeet Natak Akademy. Smt. Kamla Devi Chattopadhyay inaugurated the festival.

The relation of the deep-rooted forms of cultural activities with productive activities came out dramatically on the occasion of the commencement of a horticultural programme by IPA. The entire village gathered to plant orange and perkia (an adure bean) on about 10 acres of land. Though most of the villagers have been converted to Christianity more than 30 years ago, on this occasion they invoked the grace of the ancestors in their traditional form. They stated that during all these decades, they had discarded the traditional forms; but not they feel that if they are to go in for community based productive activities, they must draw upon the tradition to sustain the same. Also they stated that formerly they had a wrong conception that traditional form of culture were incompatible with Christianity, but of late they realised that the universality of religion could not be disharmonious with indigenous cultural forms.

## Study of indigenous form of technological development

As a logical outcome of people's growing consciousness of the value of cultural forms and practices embedded in their history and ecology, IPA has taken up several studies in the realm of science and technology at the grass-root level. It provided accommodation and other ancillary facilities to about a dozen research scholars, particularly in the field of biological sciences to conduct researches at Awangkhul and in the adjoining villages. IPA itself conducted a survey of the scope of employment of women in social forestry programme. This was presented in a seminar convened by FAO at Dehradun and has been accepted for publication. IPA undertook another survey on cane and bamboo work at Awangkhul. Based on this a Rural Marketing Centre has been established here.

In 1986 with the assistance from the Department of Science and Technology, IPA had taken up a study of people's perception of resources, and practices and social organisation of labour entering these resources. At the same time the validity of the beliefs and practices are checked through comparative studies in different techno-cultural environments or through laboratory testing. Under the overall guidance of Prof. Roy Burman, a team consisting of anthropologist, economist, cartographer, chemist, botanist, agronomist, civil engineer have been involved in this study. About 1400 botanical specimens-have been collected. While their botanical classification has been made, their local names and uses have also been recorded. Besides 33 soil samples have been collected and classified. In collaboration with Manipur University experiments are being made to generate biogas from local wastes. Studies of house types have been made in 10 villages of Manipur. Nagaland and Assam and 16 house types have been identified. The staff engineer is studying the factors contributing to their differential durability.

The fundamental problem of access to resources and management and control of the same has also been examined. IPA provided field level facilities for study of the problems of institutional finance with reference to the land system.

## Reflection about problems and prospects of IPA

While the range and magnitude of activities undertaken by IPA is impressive, the problems faced are also stupendous. Though the villagers and the personnel of IPA have taken a deliberate decision to move towards self-reliant development, it is not easy to consistently keep to the perspective and operationalise it. There are moments of doubt and there are lean periods of activities and involvement. It is difficult to say that the ideological issues, and the operational strategic consistent with the same have been worked out in all details. This is a matter of deep concern not only for Prof. Roy Burman but for all of us. One positive fact should however be noted here. Through the experience of ten years a determined leadership has come up from within the village, which understands with wider implication of the meaning of the experiment and which is capable of taking autonomous decision in the matter of IPA even in the absence of Prof. Roy Burman or myself. As however, Prof. Roy Burman and myself are too closely involved in the activities of IPA, perhaps at the appropriate moment friends who are not directly involved would like to examine in depth the wider implication of the experiments and its achievements and failures.

## REFERENCE

1. Mitra, Ashok (1976) : Presidential Address, *Symposium on Tribal Demography,* organised by Indian Association for the Study of Population of Jawaharlal Nehru University, New Delhi, Imphal, November 8 -11

# CHAPTER SEVEN
# REGIONAL HISTORY

**Regional History**

Richard Hiklyut once said, " Chronology and geography are Sunnie and Moonie, left eye and right eye of History". History deals with time (chronology) and space (geography). It is the study of the society of people of a given country or a part of a country, the habitat of a particular people. History has been classified in space frame, in the context of universal or world, continental, empire, nation states, or region within an empire or nation state. World history or universal history is of course thematic approach or base as was projected in the middle ages, was that of the universal history of the Christian nations or Muslim nation based on social categories of people, royalty, nobility and clergy. Europeans developed an Euro-centric approach in the classification of history on the geographical basis as it was claimed and accepted that Europe was the epicentre of world civilisation. Hence geographical regions like the Near East, or Middle East to denote West Asia, Far East to denote Eastern and South Eastern Asia which have been classified as East Asia, South East Asia and Southern Asia, history of continental dimensions like north America, Latin America or Central America or Oceania. European imperialism and colonialism led to the establishment of colonies and dependencies in the non-European Asia, Africa and America.

In the study of non-European countries, the European scholars devoted to the study of ancient civilisations like the Egyptian, Chinese and Indian. But with development of the history of the nation states, the urge and aspirations of the different ethnic groups and regions to incorporate their history in the mainstream history led to the history of the colonies and dependencies, former independent states merged or conquered in the empire or nation states. Thus, emerged the regional history which is the study of a region within an empire, dependent country or an independent country.

## Scope of regional history

In terms of scope, regional history deals with the study of the history of a constituent state, province, a district or a habitat of a people in an independent country. Emphasis is given to the political boundaries; but it transcends the political boundaries as it deals with ethnic and linguistic groups. Regional history is also a study of linguistic or ethnic groups based on the ethnic and linguistic habitat. The dividing line between the national history and regional history is very thin. Both are complementary; regional history deals with the micro regions within the nation states. The approach is thematic and national in outlook in the 'national' history. Whereas in the regional history, the approach is at the micro level based on the political and administrative units of the region; but it does not ignore the national history.

In Indian context, people talk of national mainstream and the regional streams in the approach to historical studies; regionalism within the gambit of nationalism or within the mainstream. Regional economic development, regional political formations, culture and civilisation of different regions have become subject of academic studies of different disciplines. In sociological study, the notions of "mainstream" and "periphery" have been popularised by the concepts of the Great Traditions and Little Traditions being emphasized at the roots of Indian civilization. This concept is focused on the Aryan mainland and non-Aryan (Mongoloid and Dravidian) peripheral indigenous ethnic groups. Out of this background the regional history has emerged to project the various smaller provinces and states. But one should be particular that regional history is complementary to the national or mainland history, because, regional history makes the national history a complete one in the case of a multi-lingual, multireligious and multi-ethnic nation like India or the United States. In a plural society, regional and ethnic history is a natural historical study.

**Growth of study of regional history**

In India, European historiographers gave an all-India pattern of history writing based on the imperial mode of writing history as introduced by James Mill's *History of India* (1819 and 1835). The purpose was to give a comprehensive history of the people of the British Indian empire. Credit should be given to the British administrators for writing local history in the district gazetteers, statistical handbooks. In the nineteenth century, Sir W. W. Hunter the Director General of Statistics gave a great impetus to this type of regional history and statistics like the *Imperial Gazetteer of India*, many provincial and district gazetteers. The British ethnographers also took part in this gigantic study. This task has been continued by the Anthropological Survey of India and the Census of India (Social Studies Department) in post Independence period.

During the national liberation struggle, the Indian historians made attempts to glorify ancient Indian culture and civilisation. These nationalist historians gave an Aryan-centric Aryabrata oriented thrust in writing a nationalist history ignoring the regional or provinces or the princely states which were once independent political formations and kingdoms. While the study of the history or princely states was encouraged by the ruling families, no importance was given by the national historians. However, the British administrators both for political purpose and personal interest wrote provincial historians. Indian scholars of the leading Universities to meet the academic requirement and research interest wrote the histories of the provinces; the examples are the' *History of Bengal* by R.C. Majumdar, Cunningham's *History of the Sikhs*. Bhadarkar's *History of the Deccan*.

North Eastern Frontier of British India is the basis of the regionalisation of North East India. The British adopted a regional approach to the North East in their policies concerning military, political, commercial and administrative affairs of the different principalities, tribes and states of the region. In 1816, the East India Company appointed an Agent to the Governor General for the North Eastern Frontier to deal with the north eastern affairs; this was the beginning of the regionalisation of the north east in political, military and commercial affairs. R.B. Pemberton's *Report on the North Eastern Frontier of British India* (1835) popularised the concept. This was further strengthened by Alexander Mackenzie in his *The History of the relations of the Government with the hill tribes of north eastern frontier of British Bengal* (1884). Sir Edward Gait who wrote *A History of Assam* (1906, 1926) provincialised the regional history.

**Regional history and Local history**

Local history is the study of a locality in a micro level study, a smaller habitat or a political formation or administrative unit. A city, a township or a village or a social group in a particular habitat can be covered by a locality based history. Local history was developed in the United

States where the 'Local' history of the states in the American Federation was given great importance in the national politics and academic world of the great country. The method adopted by the regional history and local history is almost similar. In local history and in dealing with the history of the indigenous ethnic groups, oral history or folk traditions and lore have been utilised. The history from below or the subaltern method are employed in local history. The writing of local history is dependent on the multi-methodical approach or multi-disciplinary approach ranging from the archive history to oral, folk and ethno-history. We have to mention here the village and city monographs prepared and published by the Social Studies section of the Census of India, especially from 1961 census onward. These are very important empirical and theoretical additions to the writing of local history. We have to acknoeledge the contribution of Prof. B.K. Roy Burman *in this* conceptualisation and perception of the village and township. An important example of local history *is* the *History of Kurukshetra* written by Prof. V.B. Dutt of Kurushetra University and Professor Ganda Singh's *History of Amritsar* may be also mentioned.

## Problems of regional history

Despite earlier bias for national history in Indian historiography, in recent times, regional history has gained respectability and importance due to it. Regional historiography has arrived at the national scene of history writing. Regional history has common problems or approaches like the mainstream or national history in relation to the question of sources of information like the archive data, archaeological evidences, ethnographic informations and literary information, oral traditions etc. The methodology employed *is* always multi-disciplinary: historical, sociological, *anthropological* and even folkloristic.

A great problem in regional history is in the matter of interpretation of particular historical events in the national, regional and local perspective. The skill and competence of the historian will be tested in this multi-perspective interpretation of history at three levels. There are possibilities of confrontation in this type of interpretation but it depends more on how one approaches or looks at the events, a harmonious and balanced approach is called for.

But this interpretation depends on the historiographic method adopted by the particular historians in relation to national liberation, anti-colonial struggle of the people, Marxian outlook, nationalist, chauvinist or nation building (integration) methods, It calls for a correct and rational interpretation based on the objectivity of the historian.

Multiplicity of methods and tools employed makes the interpretation a complex phenomenon. Activist interpretation makes the regional history a ground for subjectivity.

Historiography at the regional, local and micro level has assumed a global importance with the assertion of the long suppressed **Indigenous people** of the world to a rightfol place m the present world order. Regiooal history has carved out an important place in the historiography of all the leading countries of the world.

CHAPTER EIGHT

# REGIONAL HISTORIOGRAPHY OF NORTH EAST INDIA

What is a Regional History? Regional history is in a way a geographical classification of history. So a regional history is the history of a geographical unit. In the global perspective, it is continental. It may be sub-continental also in the perspective of a national or multinational state, it may be provincial or a state or a district as smaller units. However, the deciding factors in regional are both geographical and political boundaries; sometimes, it may cover ethnic, linguistic and cultural boundaries also. However, a regional history is not necessarily unconducive to the concept of an universal histor .

We have Toynbee's concept of universal history and Marx's materialistic interpretation of history which are an universal approach to the history of social development of man. Though continental classification of history like European history or African history, American history, East Asian, South East Asian is still used, they are not actually regional history in the true sense of the term. Then in the national history of a country, what is the place of regional history or local history? The dividing line between the regional history and national history is very thin. It depends upon the nature and importance of an event which occurred in a particular locality. The particular event in a locality may have a historical importance. For instance, the National Tricolour Flag was hoisted by th~ Indian National Army (I.N .A) in the obscure village of Moirang in Manipur on 14th April, 1944. At the local level, Moirang witnessed the coming of Netaji Subhas Chandra Bose's INA and raising of the flag in the soil of India. But it depends upon how an event is interpreted. The interpreter will reflect the difference or similarity of local history and national history.

However, it must be admitted that there are limitations on regional history. There is an apprehension of losing the national perspective in the over emphasis on the regional bias of a particular event. The study of regional history is very much influenced by the prevailing political boundaries of the existing political units which overlap with the past boundaries. At the same time, the ethnic and cultural boundaries are not always covered by the existing boundaries as the former transcends the latter in may cases.

Therefore, the importance of regional history lies in adding the microlevel history to the national history which appears more complete. Regionalisation of history writing strengthens the regional base of the nation building. The regional history may some time lead to regional chauvinism. Thus a regional history should not lose the national perspective.

The problems of study of regional history of North East India are due to the paucity of sources of information especially in the ancient period, the multiplicity of ethnic, linguistic and culture groups at different levels of civilization and culture which is both a problem and challenge to any student of history and the intra-regional variation in North East region which is at the same time a cultural, ethnic and political zone. Another problem is the emergence of the national history of India and the way the north east India history has to fit into it.

The north east region covering at present the seven states: Assam, Manipur, Nagaland, Tripura, Meghalaya, Mizoram and Arunachal Pradesh. Assam, with various kingdoms in ancient and medieval periods has been widely studied. The Ahoms had a strong historical sense and their chronicles known as the Buranjis are very important historical records.

The Meitei rulers of Manipur kept their chronicles known as the *Cheitharol Kumbaba.* The Tripuri rulers had *Rajmala,* a royal chronicle. Therefore, at least in these three states, the people demonstrated a sense of history. As for the Khasi states of Meghalays, the Nagas of Nagaland, the Mizos of Mizoram, the tribes of Manipur, then history writing is comparatively a recent development. The comprehensive history of the whole region has not been *completely* written. However, the colonial administrators in their various reports and monographs deal with the history of the different areas and ethnic groups. We may refer to Dr. J.P. Wade's *Account of Assam,* (1794), Francis *Hamilton's Account of Assam* (1806) as the two earliest writings on Assam and surrounding areas. They are not history as such R.B. Pemberton's Report on the *North Eastern Frontier of British India* forms the source of information on the history of the different regions. Pemberton's Report which was published in 1835, the year in which the second edition of James *Mill's History of India* was issued was a pioneering work and as such it suffers from many inadequacies. His notes and many not so well investigated remarks have left behind a trail of controversies on many historical problems of this region especially on the history of Manipur. He follows the main frame of Mill's history. It was not history but an account of the north east. His reproduction of a Shan chronicle discovered by him in Manipur deals with the history of the kingdom of Pong in Upper Burma. A large number of British, Indian and Burmese scholars had discussed the problem of identification of the kingdom of Pong with the Mogaung state of the *Mau Shans* of Upper Burma. Pemberton's Report has now become an important source of history of the region.

A few years after, a Gauhati based Christian missionary, William Robinson published *A Descriptive Account of Assam* (1841) Robinson showed the awareness of the contemporary economic, social and cultural scene in Assam and surrounding hill tribes-the economic or trade relation between the Ahoms and the hill tribes-conflicts arising out of the contradictory economic interests. His work reads quite fresh even after one and half centuries of its publication. The fact that he is a very keen ethnographic investigator is clearly indicated by his exposition on the origin of the word "Naga" whetherit was from Sanskrit "Nag" (Serpent) or "Ng" (Mountain) or "Nanga" (naked). Other "Accounts" which came after 1841 deal with small principalities or districts. We should mention William McCulloch's *An Account of the valley of Munnipore and surrounding Hill Tribes* published in 1859. McCulloch was a political Agent posted in Manipur for 23 years, who married a princess of the royal house of Maharaja Nara Singh, and settled down in Shillong after retirement and died in 1885. His remarks on the Meiteis, the Naga and Kuki tribes and his reference to the ancient society of Manipur are sketchy but significant observations. W.W. Hunter's two volumes, *Statistical Account of Assam,* based on the Gazetteer pattern reflects the colonial government's view of the political events, administrative arrangements and social situation and economic conditions in Assam and the surrounding hill areas.

## Mackenzie's history

1884 was the most significant year of colonial historiography of the north eastern India with her varied peoples and administrative units with different pasts and cultural legacies. It was in this year. Alexander Mackenzie, one of the brightest colonial administrators who served in Bengal and Burma, and who was fully aware of the British Indian administrative policy and with access to the voluminous source materials, published the history entitled on, the nineteenth century style of long title, A *History of the Relation of the Government with the Hill Tribes of North East Frontier of British Bengal,* 1884. In 1869, Mackenzie wrote *Memorandum on North East Frontier of Bengal.* And on the repeated and pressing demands from the Foreign office, this work was expanded to the volume of 1884. Mackenzie's history deals with the British policy towards all the tribes inhabiting different sectors of the north eastern region and the conquest of the tribes and gradual consolidation of the region. British were following a policy of paternalism which was well described by Kipling's *White Men's Burden.* As Mackenzie was a serving official of the Government of India who was called upon to write on an ongoing theme, he must have got some constraints. But Mackenzie who, as a colonial official strongly believed in the civilizing mission of the British imperialism, had no difficulty of projecting the colonial Government's perspective of the whole historical development.

Mackenzie who was perhaps trained in or influenced by British ideal of empiricism, was an honest chronicler of political events that shaped the relation between the British government and the north eastern frontier. He had succeeded in both objectives. But as an analyst of the historical process and the subsequent economic and social situation which emerged in the life of the region, Mackenzie had not done his job well or perhaps it was beyond the perview of his commissioned job. Therefore, what he has presented is a series of historical events and not a historical progression. There is certain basic weakness in the methodology of the colonial Indian historiography to which Mackenzie is bound. If the main task of a pioneer historian of an unknown region, was to inform and to present the ruler's point of view, Mackenzie had succeeded in presenting the facts from the colonial point of view. This historical data cannot be ignored by any student of north east Indian historiography. It is to the credit of Mackenzie that several generations of historians have been greatly influenced by his empirical data. Prof. B.K. Roy Burman, in his foreword to a recent history of Mackenzie more or less concured with the above observation.

The British administrators including the Commissioners, Chief Commissioners and Governors were persons who were deeply interested in the historical study of Assam and the surrounding region. E.A. Gait was the most renowned of all of them. The contribution of the Census of India reports, Administrative and Revenue reports are great works of research. E.A. Gait's *Progress of Historical Research in Assam*. (1896) is extremely important store house of source materials of history of north east region. E.A. Gait published his *History of Assam* in 1906. There is no other work covering wide canvass from the ancient to the twentieth century, and surrounding hill principalities. What V.A. Smith's work is to study of ancient Indian history, Gait's is to the history of north east region. It is a great contribution to the development of historiography of the region. Gait's history aroused both appreciation and critical comments. But Gait's history utilized the available source materials at the turn of the century to reconstruct the history of ancient Assam, which was very sketchy. and only fifteen pages were devoted to it.

The medieval history of the Ahom kingdom, the surrounding principalities of the Koch, Kachari, Jaintia has been properly dealt with by utilizing the *Ahom Buranjis*. Perhaps, the medieval section is the best written part of

Gait's monumental works. The decline of the Ahoms, Moamaria rebellions, British intervention in eighteenth century and non interference in early part of nineteenth century and the Anglo Burmese war and the Treaty of Yandaboo and gradual British expansion in the nineteenth century have been well described. The neighbouring state of Manipur, Khasi and Jaintia State, Cachar, Naga Hills and Arunachal tribes have also been covered. After twenty one years, in 1926, the second edition came out and he had tried to incorporate the critical observations on his works including Vidya Vinod Bhattarcharja's *Critical study of Gait's History.* After Gait's work, emerged the publication of specialised study of different periods of Assam's history. Subsequent works have greatly improved upon Gait's history but it continues to be a great reference works on the region in India and abroad.

As a sequence to Gait's history was KL. Barua's *Early History of Kamarupa* (1933) which dealt with the ancient history of Assam and the region up to the fifteenth century. Barua had utilized the Greek, Roman and Chinese sources over and above the Indian literary sources, which were greatly reinforced by the archaeological evidences, epigraphy, sculpture and architectural remains. The Indian perspective of the regional history has been presented in this work of Barua. The early medieval history, dealing with religious aspects are a good contributions to the introducing of the history of the period. Barua's work utilized most of the avilable local sources and the researches of the contemporary scholars.

**Reid's History of Border Areas**

Robert Reid, a Governor of Assam trying to continue the tradition of Alexander Mackenzie, published his *History of Area Bordering Assam* in 1942, based on the official documents to which he had a ready access. He deals with the hill states and districts like, Manipur, Tripura, Khasi states, Garo Hills, Naga Hills, Lushai Hills and Sadiya and Banpara tracts. This book is really not a history but a compilation of relevant official correspondences to depict the political events of the districts or states concerned. Reid wanted to make the official documents narrate their own history. But the book lacks a central theme and a chronological frame. It is a historical account of events chosen at almost at random and put together, Therefore, the regional pattern found in Mackenzie is absent though inter-regional units are depicted. Even the Government's policy on the macro-regional level is never indicated. Colonial administrator's task and chronicler's task are not completely done. However, this is a compilation of documents for administrative history of the region. As it was published during the Second World War and from Shillong, the book did not receive any notice from the historians. This book did not have a history for twenty years. Only after India's dispute with China over the eastern border blew up, this book came to be noticed by the officials of the External Affairs Ministry and other interested in the MacMohon Line and related boundary issues.

After India's independence, S.K. *Bhuyan's Anglo Assamese Relation,* (1948) was a remarkable work in the eighteenth century history of Assam and British conquest of Ahom Kingdom. S.K. Bhuyan's contribution as a historian and a promoter of historical studies was really great. It was he who with a good academic training in historiography brought the regional historiography of North East to the Indian historical scene. He as the Director of the **Antiquarian and Historical Studies,** Assam based at Gauhati was responsible for the publication of a large number of Ahom chronicles known as the *Buranji* including *Tungkhungiya Buranji* in English and others in Assamese. G.C. Barua had earlier published the *Ahom Buranji* in 1935. Bhuyan, as an academician and active educational actvist was responsible for various academic enterprises in the region.

The social and cultural history was covered by N.N. Vasu's *Social History of Kamarup* in three volumes, B.K. Barua's *Cultural History of Assam*, B.K. Kakati's *Mother Goddess Kamakhya*. S.K. Chatterjee's *Krita Jana-Kriti or contribution of Indo-Mongoloid to Indian culture* (1950, 1974). S.K. Chatterjee's Banikanta *Kokati Memorial Lecture: The place of Assam in the civilizction of India* (1954). In ancient history P.C. Choudhury's *A History of the Civilization of the people of Assam to the twelfth century A.D.* (1960) is a monumental contribution.

Professor H.K. Borpujari's *Assam in the Days of the company and Problems of Hill Tribes of the North Eastern Frontier* in three volumes have critically analysed the policy of the British colonial Government in the nineteenth century and have brought the history of the hill areas of the region up to 1962. Professor Borpujari adopts very scientific approach and his efforts to promote historical study in the region are highly commendable. His contribution to regional historiography, both as a chronicler and analyst of historical events is really great. Professor Amalendu Guha's Marxian approach to Assam history has given a completely new dimension to the historiography of the region. His *Planter Raj to Swaraj* dealing with the parliamentary politics and resultant changes in Assam has been widely appreciated.

The studies on different units, Manipur, Nagaland, Cachar, Mizoram, Meghalaya and Tripura have been in the recent years, profused and have not been covered in this paper.

The study of regional history at the Post-Graduate and Graduate classes was initiated in Gauhati University. It was followed by Dibrugarh University, the North East Hill University and Jawaharlal Nehru University Centre at Imphal (now Manipur University). The study of the history, culture, ethnography has been promoted by the vast research programme of these universities.

CHAPTER NINE

# HISTORY AS AN INTER-CULTURE ENCOUNTER

## Experience of North East India

History is a story of civilisation; it is an account of the evolution of human society and culture. History is also an encounter of cultures of different races and ethnic groups which produced both integration and assimilation. North East India is a great example of inter-culture encounter.

India's North East is a mosaic of cultures and races. It has been the meeting place of various cultures, religious, ethnic and linguistic groups. It is a place where India meets South East Asia and Inner Asia as the various ethnic groups of the Southern Mongoloid migrated to the region in different periods of history. These are the Austroloid (or Austric) like the Khasi and Jaintia, the Tibeto- Burman (or the Indo-Mongoloid) groups, namely, the widely spread Bodos (Dimas a, Kachari, Koch, Mech, Garos, Tripuri etc.), the Meiteis of Manipur, the Nagas of Nagaland, Assam and Manipur, the Mizos of Mozoram, Kuki-Chins and various Tibetan related tribes of Arunachal Pradesh like the Monpas, Daflas, Serdukpen, Adi, Apatanis, the Gallong, Singphos etc. Then there are the Indo-Aryan people like the Assamese and Bengalis and other Indian immigrants.

## Two cradles of civilization

There are two cradles of civilization and human creativity in the North East. The Brahmaputra valley in Assam and Imphal valley in Manipur where grew up states and civilization. In the Brahmaputra valley, there were Hinduised Bodo States in ancient times, Pragjyotish and Kamarup, the Ahom kingdom in the medieval period. Then came the British. The Aryans migrated to the region, and spread the Hindu religion and culture among the Mongoloid peoples; Hinduism was followed by Buddhism. The Turko-Afghans and Mughals invaded the north east India and brought the Muslim migrants and the Islamic religion. The Ahom Tais came as conquerors but were absorbed by Hinduism in Assam. The British colonial rulers brought Christinianity. Hinduism was more or less confined to the plains. Islam was also confined to the plains. They did not penetrate into the hills. Christianity was spread to the hills and among the tribes. The Hindu plainsmen did not accept Christianity. Buddhism was spread both in the hills and plains in small numbers. There were inter ethnic interactions on social, religious and cultural matters. These elements of culture and religion coexist. Colonialism imposed a common rule over them, but the tribals, mostly non-Hindu and non-Muslim were alienated from the plainsmen.

In Manipur valley, which is the main gateway of India to South-East Asia, the Meiteis built up a state and society with a thriving culture. The various elements of the Tibeto-Burman with some Tai and admixtures have contributed to the evolution of the cultural heritage of Manipur. The Naga and Kuki Chin tribes have also contributed to it. Meiteis professed the indigenous or traditional religion; then came Hinduism and Sanskritization. Some Buddhist elements were brought in; Islam came with the migration of Muslims in Manipur since the 17th century. British colonial rule brought Christianity which was accepted by the hill tribes.

The communities have kith and kin across the border in the neighbouring countries of South Asia, Bangladesh and even Tibet. North East India passed through a process of cultural and social integration and assimilation.

## Colonial interlude

With their conquest of North East India (1826-1891), the British applied the usual rules and norms of colonialism in their administration over the North East. The hill tribes who came into violent conflict with them were completely alienated and separated from the Hindu peoples of the plain, the Brahmaputra valley, the Imphal valley and the Barak valley. They took up the **Whitemen's Burden** to civilise the hill tribes of the region who were brought under the colonial protective umbrella. Westernisation and modernisation through Western education, Christianity and Christian mission who came to convert the hill tribes. But they did not bring about the upliftment of the economic condition of the people whose lands and natural resources had been exploited by the colonial rulers. The Second World War brought tremendous changes to the people of North-East, both hills and plains. They suffered the ravages of the great war and were exposed to the western destructive military technology and a great chapter in modernisation was started. The colonial rulers, posed and acted as the saviour and protector of the hill tribes. The hill tribes were isolated or seperated and converted to Christianity. This phenomenon of social distance and religious differentiation brought about a dichotomy between the peoples and communities in respect of their religion and language. The difference of language, religion and race was given an exaggrated dimension. The cleavage covers cultural relationship. The Christianity, however, brought the liberalising force in tribal society.

## Cultural pluralism

The leaders of Indian national liberation struggle and

the founding fathers of the Indian Constitution visualised an egalitarian society with a policy of protecting the weaker sections like the tribals and analogous peoples. They are described as the Scheduled Tribes and liberal social policy to uplift them has been in operation. It has led to tremendous social, educational, economic and political development among the tribal peoples of North-East India. India believes in ethnic and cultural pluralism under the garb of democracy, socialism and secularism. Yet there were unrest, agitation, insurgencies and rebellions, among the peoples of the NorthEast. To meet their ethnic aspiration, preserve their cultural identity and develop their social and economic life, new states were created. Thus, emerged the seven sisters, Assam, Nagaland, Manipur, Meghalaya, Tripura, Mizoram and Arunachal Pradesh. The Government of India tries to accommodate these movements within the gambit of autonomy and self-government under the Indian Constitution. The structures or political formations, called the states, were established to protect the marginalised peoples who would be well protected in their social, economic and cultural relationship with the rest of the country. In social and cultural terms these movements are a search for ethnic and cultural identity.

Yet the various groups in the North-East face two problems: Problem of forging a common regional identity in the context of India's polity and capitalist economy: another problem is the necessity of resolving the inter-regional economic, social and cultural differences Regional cooperation has been forged to face the external forces like large-scale immigration from Bangladesh and Nepal on the slogan of preserving cultural and ethnic and inter-regional cultural identity. However, serious attempts have been made by the central governments, including many voluntary organisations to document, preserve and communicate various art form of the region. This will go along way in forging a common cultural affiliation among the people. At the political level, the national political leadership has tried to accommodate the ethnic aspirations, the economic forces are so powerful that the region as a whole is a victim of internal colonialism. Except the state of Assam, all other states are highly subsidized by the central government. This is a great investment of the nation in accommodating the marginal cultural groups and nationalities into the Indian Union. This is in a way, the extension of the policy of cultural pluralism; unity in diversity. The feeling of the fear of the great Indian multitude; political economic and cultural hegemony from mainland India still persists. Their survival as cultural entities depend on their capacity to protect the tribal land, forests, ecology and environment. Cultural autonomy should accompany the political autonomy and self-government. In this, the state of Nagaland with constitutional guarantee for protection of land, natural resources and customary institutions have given the best model of autonomy and self-government in India. However, the Naga insurgency continues. Other non-tribal insurgencies like the Assamese and the Meitei also continue.

Lastly, an Inter-culture encounter in time and space has produced integration and assimilation in the form of Sanskritization of the plain dewellers of the North-East; Christianity has forged Christian brotherhood after the indigenisation of the Christian missions in the North-East among the hill tribes. Some of the insurgents adopt Christianity as their slogan. But the recent ethnic clash among the Kukis and Nagas of Manipur despite their common affiliation to Christianity also show that the religious affinity has been overwhelmed by the ethnic and cultural identities of the respective communities. Hinduism which was once thought to be an integrating factor, has failed to restrain the Hindu Meiteis of Manipur from revolting against the government. There is also a process of desanskritization in Manipur and de-christianization in Meghalaya. The Meitei revivalist movement for going back to their indigenous pre-Hindu Sanamahi religion is quit vocal and strong. The Seng Khasi movement is for going back and the revival of the Khasi traditional religion is going on for a few decades in Meghalaya.

The North-East India is passing through a crisis of cultural indentity. It is also clear that the problem of the tribal and the analogous people of North- East India is not peculiar to the region alone. Many of the indigenous peoples of Asia face similar problems under the tremendous global economic and political changes. The voyage for the resolution of the human problems through the control of and communion with nature has to continue. The inter-cultural encounter will also continue towards a better world.

CHAPTER TEN

# STATE FORMATION IN NORTH EAST INDIA

## I

Origin and process of formation of states has been the recurrent theme of some of the most significant historical, philosophical and scientific writings from the classical Greek thinkers like Plato and Aristotle down to the sociologists and political anthropoligists of the present time. In common parlance, "the state is a geographically limited segment of human society united by a common obedience to a single sovereign" : it is also a human community of people which successfully claims the monopoly of legitimate use of physical force within a given territory. The State has been regarded as a social institution with unique basic features, namely, "population, territoriality, legitimacy and sovereignty". Below these outward features, are the complexities which are inherent in the structure of the society itself. Therefore, the enquiry into origin of the state is greatly linked up with the study of social function and cultural evolution of the people concerned.[1] According to sociologists, "the state is essentially a social organisation which is given expression to the existing relations in a society and to ideas pertaining to power, authority, force, justice, property and many other phenomena."[2] The Greek and Roman Philosophers, Plato, Aristotle, Stoics and Epicureans regarded the state as

'Coterminus' with society itself.[3] Ibn Khaldun of Tunis in his *Introduction to History* (1377) propounded the Arab idea of historiography which is still relevant to modern historiography. He wrote about the social structural factors as differentiated in nomadic and sedentary cultures and the dynamic relations between these two kinds of cultures and societies. It is this perspective of dynamic relations between the two societies that provided the idea of the motive force in the historical process. This is a view which has been adopted by the modem sociologists of the "conflict school" of the formation process.[4]

## II
## Origin of the State:

### Machiavelli: The Prince

Machiavelli was the first European modern thinker who perceived the state purely from the secular point of view as represented by the monarch and "divested of moralistic, theological and metaphysical attitudes". Ethics was separated from politics, Machiavelli in the Prince analysed the nature of the state, the goals of government which are a portrait of a nation state which arose in Europe. Lord Acton writes somewhere that "the authentic interpreter of Machiavelli is the whole of later history". Jean Bodin of France who witnessed the turmoils in his country in the absence of a strong state, like Ibn Khaldun and Machiavelli, was a protagonist of a strong dynastic state. Bodin's theory of origin of state and government is essentially like that of Khaldun that state arises out of conflict.

### Contractualists

Thomas Hobbes (1588-1679) was the first English thinker who in the Leviathan, propounded the Social Contract Theory of the state according to which men in order to escape from the anarchy of the state of nature made a contract among them to create a totalitarian despotic state. His compatriot, John Locke proposed a Social Contract Theory for the creation of a republican state. However, J. J. Rousseau's ideal state of nature was a highly romanticised society. Men made contract among themselves and surrendered their ego to the society and not to the state. The general will of the society was, thus, evolved and it governed the legitimate government as the agent of the society. The German idealist school projected the state as the ultimate realisation of the idea which is the motive force of history. Hegel was the high priest of the Idealist school who pleaded for an absolutist German state. "State is march of God on earth", Hegel wrote.

**Marxian view**

Karl Marx and Frederick Engels in the *Communist Manifesto* (1848) declared that the state was a structure created by the power wielding exploiters to promote their interests and oppress the peasants and workers. They did not give a theoretical exposition on the formation and origin of state as an institution till the later part of the nineteenth century. It was Frederick Engels who developed the concept of emergence of the State. The American anthropologist, L.H. Morgan in the *Ancient Society* (1877) which was based on the empirical data of some American Indian tribes, revealed that primitive society was communities (community ownership of resources) lacking in private property economic classes of despotic ruler. However, increased productivity or economic activities led to the increased trade and emergence of private property and class of rich who acquired more from the community's pool of resources and the poor who got lesser from the common pool. Ultimately, the primitive state structure was created by the propertied class to manage the complex relationship and to protect the interests of the rich and the powerful class. The materialistic conception of history according to Marx and Engels, can explain the transition from primitive society to civil society. Frederick Engels in his

*Origin of Family, Private Property and the State* (1884) explains the process in an elaborate way, something in the following way. "Certain primitive society had improved the technological means of production, the surplus of which was traded and the process was expanded; society perforce changed from a production for use economy to a production of commodities. Unearned increments arose due to differences in efficiency in supply and demand, the activities of middlemen; thus, with the rise of private difference in wealth, economic class appeared."[5]

Engels summed up the whole explanation: "The state is, therefore, by no means a power forced on society from without; just a little is it". Rather it is a product of society at a certain stage of development; it is the admission that the society has become entangled in an insoluble contradiction with itself, that it has split into irreconcilable antagonism classes with conflicting economic interest, might not consume themselves and society in fruitless struggle, it became necessary to have a power seemingly standing above society that would alleviate the conflict and keep it within bounds of "Order" and this power, arisen out of society but placing itself above it, and alienating itself more and more from it, is the state."[6] This is the economic genesis of the state. From their materialist beginning the classes gradually became social and ultimately political when the rich erected a structure of permanent force to protect the class interests. The State, according to the Marxist, view is a special instrument of repression, of the propertied class.

Lenin in his *State and Revolution*, pointed out the historical role and meaning of the state and reemphasised that Marxism revealed the necessity of destruction of both the class system and the state, for, the state represents and protects only the propertied classes.[7] The distinguishing features of the state according to Engels are the territory, establishment of a public power, imposition of taxes, introduction of public debts and authority for the bureaucracy of the State.[8]

**Positivists**

Auguste Comte (1798-1857), the father of sociology also thought that the state was coterminus with society. Herbert Spencer (1820-1903) who was an exponent of social Darwinism regarded society as a system analogous to structure, functioning and specialization of parts of its living organism. Spencer attributed the rise of the state of warfare with important development in legal, economic and religious organisation. Warfare may select the stronger and the more efficient. This is, however, no clear distinction between state and non-state society. They project a militant state in which the individuals are subordinate to the authority. The conflict theory and social Darwinism are combined by Spencer.

## III
## Process of Formation

State Formation is the process of evolution, growth or constitution of a people or a social group or groups occupying a geographical region into a political society through different stages and phases of social and economic formations. But there is not a definite explanation of the process of formation of the states. Ronald Cohen in *State Foundation: A Controlled Comparison in Origin of State; The Anthropology of political Evolution* (1978) observes, "There is no clear cut or simple set of causal statement that explains the phenomenon of stat formation. The formation of state is a funnel like progression of interactions in which a variety of pre-state structures responding to different determinats of change are found by other unresolvable conflicts to choose additional and more complex laws of political hiearchy. Once the particular solution is hit upon, the structural features of the adaptation and benefits cause these polities to converge culturally and socially into early states." However, he further observes, :What is lacking is an agreed upon model or explanatory paradigm that puts these correlates together with the set of process that produces states from the pre-states." [9] The absence of a generally accepted single theory or hypothesis is due to the variation in the factors that led to the emergence of states. It will be worthwhile to have an awareness of the typology of states under discussion.

Typology of states can be established according to the manner of the weilding of the power of the state, the time and peculairities of the emergence of the states. For the study of the state formation, states have been classified into early states and modem states as done by Henry Claessen and Peter Skalnik in the *Early State* (1978). The early states are simple, non-industrialized and pre-capitalistic whereas the modem states are complex, industrialized and developing. Morton H. Fried (1978) states that "The political state is not only a structure not merely emergence from a long process of demographic, ecological and economic development but as a source of revoltionary transformation of culture in general." He further continues, : "Fundamental to this conception is the notion that the state is something more than a formally organised society or even an aggregate of institutions and apparatus of social control at some specified level of complexity." [10]

Fried classifies the states into two types: namely, the pristine state and the secondary state. This typology of states on the basis of natural evolution or external sponsorship is important. Pristine states pose difficulties in tracing their origin. Pristine states like the "primitive" society are simple, early, original, primary and lacking in development. Morton Fried (1967) explains the evolution of the pristine states through three stages with corresponding social formations:

1. Egalitarianism : Band and tribal society
2. Ranked Society : Chiefdom
3. Stratified Society : State

We may recall Morgan's assumption that stratification was the main spring for the foundation of political society. Fried thinks that such a stratification in society should be viewed more as a rank and it should be better described as ranked society. According to him, it is more a division of labour and not a division of properties. Evidence of pristine states is lacking. It is mostly from archaeology that evidence for this type of state is derived. However, pristine states are found in Mexican autonthonous political formations and tribal North East India. Secondary states are formed due to the pressures from the existing states and which often use parts or all of the organisation of some prior states as the model of emulation or improvement. Secondary states may also be called sponsored states. Sometimes, there is confusion between pristine and secondary state formations. Studies on state formations are mostly on secondary state formations while pristine state formations are based on the transformation of tribal society formations to state.

Process of formation of states has been explained in different theories on the subject. E.R. Service in his Classical and Modem theories of the Origin of the government,[11] has presented the existing theories into categories of theories: I. Conflict Theories, and II. Integration Theories. According to Conflict Theories, the individual conflicts in the prestate societies have been a) the basis of two categories of theories, (b) the Social Contract, and (c) Social Darwinism. Social Contract theory explains the nature of the state rather than the process of state formation. Even Social Darwinism has little relevance to the problem of stateformation.

The Conflict Theory assumes a greater importance when it is applied to explain the intra-societal conflicts. According to the Marxian view which is the best representative of this theory, the emergence of the state proceeds on the basis of intra-societal conflict in the form of "class struggle". Engels gives four stages of social development:[12]

1. Primitive Communism
2. Emergence of Private property
3. Formation of Social and Economic Class
4. Emergence of the state

Primitive communism was the first stage of social formation in which there was no private property, no trade and commerce, no classes of rich and poor and no despotic ruler. The development of technology and its gradual improvement led to the increased productivity of economic activities and the community's common resources of property increased. The individuals started acquiring things from the community's pool of resources and it was legitimized and the private property emerged. The creation of private property led to the concentration of the property into the hands of small but strong groups of peoples which ultimately resulted into the emergence of social and economic classes. The dominant class stated devising means to perpetuate their control over their private property and subjugate the others who had been deprived of access to the common resources. In order to manage the socio-economic affairs of men and to protect the interests of the dominant class, a military power was created and out of this a structure of the productivity due to technological development, surplus products were created. And trade in those surplus commodities resulted in the change of the economy for consumption or subsistence to production of commodities for exchange. This type of economy necessitated the growth of middlemen, entrepreneur, and capital. The class structure so evolved is perpetuated through the state. According to Engels, the transformation of this structure was through the stages as stated above: primitive communism, tribal to feudal and to the bourgeoisie. He also mentions the oriental epoch based on the Asiatic Mode of production which grew up in the Orient. In this context, Amalendu Guha's explanation is very appropriate. "No tribe leaped to statehood while it was still at its pristine state, when it still lacked sedentary agricultural populations, is degree or division of labour and social stratification. Statehood emerged only when a community was either itself capable of producing a surplus sufficient for the maintenance of a non-producing public authority, or of systematically appropriating as tribute the requisite surplus form a subject community or both"[13] Guha continues, " The transformation of the surplus producing community into state took place when the leading families who had the customary monopoly of supplying important public functionaries began to realise that their capability could also be utilized to promote their own specific economic interests. In other words, the process of state formation started when they began to realize that they formed an interest group, a class in the making."[14]

According to the Integration Theory, the state is the supreme apparatus above the kinship organization to provide benefits to the members of the society. This is created to control and supervise (i) the redistribution system, namely, production, distribution, consumption and long distance trade, (ii) war organization to provide security of life and property of the members of the society within and without the state; (iii) public works undertaking, specially water control system to benefit agricultural production and agrarians. This theory does not explain the process of the formation of the states.

According to the External Conflict or conquest theory as propounded by R.L. Carniero, in hisAn *External Conflict Theory of State Origin* (1978), the population growth of a society produced pressure on agriculture resources which led to the competitions, armed or unarmed, in the form of warfare which necessitated the formation of war organization resulting into a dominant ruling group and subjected groups which paid tribute to the dominant group. The administrative need to regulate all these complex situation led to the creation of a centralized organization called the state.

It is now clearly seen that the states, both pristine and secondary, do not just happen; they are the result of the conflict, struggle and other conditions of change inherent in a society that creates a new authority structure where none previously existed. We may note the role of technological development which contributed to state formation.[15] The invention of agriculture, increase in population, shortage of land for production, warfare as a mechanism of political evolution, taxation, social stratification, ecological competition, slavery, theocratic rule and urbanism are characteristics associated with stage formation.[16]

With regard to the actual process of formation of pristine states, there are no records in the west except in archaeology. Mesopotamia represents a case of pristine state of urban nature.[17] But tribal African tribal north east India and Meso-American state like the Incas provide the instances of these original states.

Barbara Price refers to two processes of Secondary state formation.[18] One is the historical succession from pre-existing states, pristine or secondary, the second is the expansion of the existing states into areas inhabited by population, but not covered by any organised states.

The first is the direct process in the form of political incorporation or massive takeover and control over the resources. Thus, the interactions between states and non-states are socio-eco system's support for the production system, trade including long distance trade, War and Urban development. Samir Amin (1979) gives a great importance to the role of long distance trade and associated infrastructure and capability of a society to promote trade as a major contributing factor to the strengthening of the ruling elite and growth of states, both pristine and secondary.

State formation as a process of cultural evolution has been highlighted by Elan R. Service (1975), "Creation of culture is a great human achievement by the use of which the society tames and governs their members, create and maintain their complex social organization. Culture has technological, economic, religious, artistic and recreational functions. All of these depend on the ability of the political aspects of culture to integrate and protect the society. A Society grows or declines depending on its ability to preserve the authority." [19]

These major factors, contributory to the emergence to statehood as given by H.J.M. Claessen and Peter Skalnik,[20] are the population growth and population pressure, war, the threat of war or conquest and raids, conquest, progress in production and the promotion of surplus, tribute, affluence, ideology and legitimisation, and the influence of the existing states.[21]

## IV

### The Indian studies

Regarding the Indian studies on State formation, Romila Thapar remarks that "Theories on the earliest formation of States in India have been few and generally simplistic. There is none of the conceptual richness which characterises the discussion on state formation in Africa or Meso America, partly perhaps, because the latter have drawn on ideas relating to the early states among political anthropoligists." [22] This poverty of theory according to her, is due to the obsession with a single image of the oriental despotism and Marxian Asiatic Mode of production which is enthusiastically projected by western writers despite its lack of empirical data to support it.[23] Even the studies on political institutions in early India which were influenced by Indian nationalism assumed the existence of the concept of the state but rarely analysed the process by which the state formation came about.[24] It was Surajit C. Sinha who initiated the study on the subject with anthropological method and historical data in his *State Formation and Rajput Myth in Tribal Central India* (1962). This pioneering work inspired further investigations into the question of the state formation[25] though the progress is slow. Since his publication, western anthropoligists have further develcped different theories on state formation: Cohen, Service, Fried, Claessen and Skalnik, and Godelier may be named. A decade after, K.S. Singh published two papers, *State Formations in Tribal Society: Some Preliminary Observation (1972)*[26] based on the tribal states in Chhotanagpur region and a Study in *State Formation among the Tribal Communities* (1974).[27] *The Early State* (1978) which has been referred to above is an anthology of twenty two case studies of state formation including some studies on Indian state: *The Mauryan State* by Sudharshan Seniverathe and *The Dimasa State* by Sofia A. Martina. Hermann Kulke did two good works. *Early State Formation and Royal Legitimation in Tribal Areas of Eastern India* (1978) in Orissa[28] by Jagannath Kult and Gajapati Konigtum (1979),[30] B. Stein's Peasant *State and Society in Medieval South India* (1980) is another contribution.[31] Another landmark was the workshop on *Tribal Polities and State Systems in Pre colonial Eastern andNorth Eastern India* in July, 1981, which was sponsored by the Centre for Study in Social Science in Calcutta under the leadership of Surajit C. Sinha again. Significant contributions were made by eminent social scientists and historians in this workshop. This academic exercise at Calcutta was the turning point and following it a number of studies on state formation specially in North East India came out. S.C. Sinha (ed) *The Tribal Polities and State Systems in Precolonial Eastern and North Eastern India* (1987) dealing with the major theoretical issues and several case studies on Manipur, Sikkim, laintia, Ahom, Mizo Cachar is a monumental work,[32] Almost simultaneously Romila Thapar in her Heras Memorial Lecturs (1980) enquired into the state formation in early India. This lecture is published in the form of a book *From Lineage to State* (1984). This work deals with the evolution of the social formation into state in ancient India in the first millenium B.C. in northern India. Romila Thapar's work is a major addition to the literatures on state formation both on the theoretical and empirical levels. Her survey of different theories is extremely knowledgeable. State formation according to her, is a "complex process in which a range of factors may be crucial and may apply to varying situations. Therefore there will be no single factor of state formation. The form of the states would vary according to the nature of its origin." She differentiated between the primary and secondary states. Her work is concerned with the emergence of the primary state; the transformation of the lineage society to the state. A lineage is "a corporate group of unilinial kin with a formalized system of authority with rights and duties and the geneological relationship as the binding factor." Romila Thapar indicates that "the Vedic period saw a change from the lineage system (Rig Vedic) to a combined lineage and territorial (later Vedic) and to sharper stratification (Post Vedic) of the Chieftainship (Chiefdom) which was germinal to the State formation". Romila Thapar further emphasises the relevancy of the study of state formation to Indian history as the process of state formation is a continuing one throughout the country as new areas are being brought into the State system.[33] It will be necessary to study the pre state structure to have insight in the whole process.

The workshop at Calcutta based on the paper of Barun De (Concepts and Issues) and several case studies of State formations has identified certain common elements in the process of State formation in precolonial and medieval India. The workshop made an eleven points formulation which has been referred to in the learned papers by J.B. Bhattacharjee on *Tripuri State and Dimasa State*. Because of its significance, *it is* reproduced, despite the possible monotony of repetition.

(i) The tribal formations underwent transformation with

the emergence of private property, when the tribal societies were stratified into classes in terms of differentiated land holding and the extent of political dominance that strength ened the position of the traditional chiefs at clan/tribe level.

(ii) The sphere of political dominance of a chief was extended either by subduing the neighbouring tribes/ class/communities or by direct territorial conquest or by their voluntary submission to his protective authority.

(iii) The authority was further strengthened by leading the people in War path either for offensive or for defensive purposes and it continued to be unquestioned at least at the formative stage, in cases were the state came into existence through military adventurism.

(iv) The ruling chiefs succeeded in developing a centralised administration with an elaborate defense structure and the means to appropriate surplus through a hierarchical state order.

(v) The introduction of more developed agricultural technology to ensure increased production, and the production control on the part of the ruler could be an essential pre-condition for a centralized state authority.

(vi) The families with traditions of administrative proficiency and artisans and peasants were induced to immigrate and settle in the territory.

(vii) The process of Hinduisation/Sanskritization and the role of the Brahmins in establishing the divine origin of the ruler helped the legitimization of the assumed status of the latter'and its consolidation, and the myths that were created in the process resulted in the universalization of the culture.

(viii) The adoption of the language and culture of the majority in the territory's population by the ruling family and the aristocracy enlisted loyalty and support of that dominant revenue paying group.

(ix) The rulers emerged as the champions of their new faith and patrons of the culture and language of their subjects.

(x) The matrimonial connections maintained with the ruling houses in order states with almost similar ethno-cultural traditions evoked mutual support and raised them in the estimation of their subjects.

(xi) The diplomatic relations with more powerful neighbours were essential either to guarantee political existence in the face of expanding influences of such neighbours or to pacify the disgruntled elements within the state.[34]

Professor B.K. Roy Burman in a recent paper entitled *Rethinking on State Formation and Process in Tribal Areas: A Rapid Overview* (1987) does not agree with the Calcutta formulation. He observes "This formulation is an unassorted admixture of aspects relating to primary and secondary state formations. The last item of this formulation clearly indicates that the states that come into existence in tribal areas were mostly sponsored states. The aspects described at (items) VI to X are basically exogenous processes. The aspects described at (items) I to V may or may not take place. Even in the case of state formation through indigenous formation, the aspects described at (items) I to V constitute an inventory; it is not inevitable that all of them would be found together. Besides, the presence of all of them does, not necessarily imply that a full fledged state has come into existence. These observations deserve a careful examination.

He, further, comments, "The formulation seems to be based on confusion about several categories of phenomenon: (i) State and government, (ii) chiefship and state, (iii) ranked society, stratified society and class society. It is differentiated homage, tribute, rent, revenue and tax from one another in tracing the laws of the state formation and state process."

He suggests that "at the level of methodology, for gaining an insight into the state process, it is also necessary to consider the historical ecology of the failure of emergence of state structure and of oscillation from one type of state like structure to another through intermediate formation in some parts of the country."

The eleven point-fonnulations are the common features in the process of the state fonnation of the secondary states. As pointed out earlier there is no single agreed upon theoretical formulation, Comments of Professor Roy Bunnan on the lack of differentiation between state the government, chiefship and state, ranked society, stratified society and class society are clarified when one goes through the excellent papers presented in the workshop for instance, Prof. A Guha's Ahom Political Systems or Professor Bhattacharjee's Dimasa State. His reference to the failure of the emergence of the state structure even after the formation of private property and trade, has been corroborated by Professor Amalendu Guha who informs that among the Apatanis of Arunachal Pradesh who had developed a degree of private property rights, no state or state like structure emerged. "Segmentary primitive societies in pre state situation were not transfonned into states overnight even by the magic wand of property. "[35] However, Prof. Roy Burman's rethinking on the irrelevance of nation state in the contemporary global context and the constraints on the state structure ought to be studied in greater depth.

With regard to the study of the non state segmentary societies, there is unanimity to give the thrust on this aspect. As the state formation is an ongoing process in the contemporary Indian political system, the role of ethnicity in the evolution of autonomous states within Indian political system has been well known. Gangmumei Kabui, in his Ethnicity and State Fonnation in North East India (1985) pointed out the ethnic factor in the formation of autonomous state structure in North East India like Nagaland and Mizoram. K.S. Singh in a paper submitted to A.S.I. Seminar in Shillong (1987), Ethnicity and Polity Fonnation in Tribal India, points out that though the Indian constitution does not recognise ethnicity, in actual process of fonnation of states to fulfil the ethnic aspirations, ethnicity has become a criteria for the formation of states in contemporary India.

**North east India: Dimasa state**

The processes of the formation in north east India both pristine and secondary stats, has been a subject matter of great academic exercise among the social scientists and the historians. The first systematic study was carried out by a Soviet sociologist, Sofia A. Maretina in the Kachari state. The character of early state like formation in the hill districts of North East India which was based on C.A. Soppit, An Historical and Descriptive Account of the Kachari Tribes in the North Cachar Hills, Shillong 1885 which is included in Claessen and Skalnik, The early State (1978). Based on the data of Maretina, Claessen in Early State, A structural approach, categorised the Kachari State as a typical state. Maretina points to six characteristics of the state like formations in north east India: 1. Slow rate and incompleteness of the process of class formation in early state. And hence pre class character of these states, 2. The basic preservation of traces of the class structure in the hierarchy of the social strata. 3. The importance of the role played in the stablization of state and strengthening of the dominant position of the privileged social strata, 4. The indispensability of the contacts with advanced state systems of the contacts with advanced state systems to provide the required attributes of a state structure, 5. The greater role played by the economic factor then in the case of more advanced stage of development, as reflected in the difference of evolutions between the hill areas and the plain areas, 6. The transfer to the plains as an indispensable factor in the formation of the early state.[36]

J.B. Bhattacharjee in his study of the *Dimasa State* (1984), with a greater command and access to more authentic empirical data, both historical and sociological, comments on Maretina's analysis thus: "It should, however, be said in favour of Maretina that she could build up an excellent case study on the basis of extremely scanty data at her command and that her basic assumption and conclusion remain valid in spite of additional and more authenticated historical evidences that one is able to cite, primarily due to her strong theoretical base and a sound understanding of the historical and sociological processes"[37] Bhattacharjee made an almost independent study of the formation of the Dimasa State in three phases of their long history in their respective location of their political headquarters at Sadiya, Dimapur, Maibong and Khaspur : the early phase (Sadiya and Dimapur); Intermediate phase (Maibong in North Cachar Hills) and final phase (Khaspur in Cachar Valley). The Dimasa state that was finally developed at Khaspur was a monarchy of the Indian pattern. The governing factors for the transformation of the Dimasa social formation to the state are sanskritization, conquest or war against the invaders, adoption of settled agriculture, use of Bengali language in administration and retention of the original tribal identity. The social transformation of the Dimasa to statehood was of course marked by the disintegration of their clan structure and substitution by stratification and hierarchical social organization in the Hindu model.

**The Tripuri state**

Credit should be given to Professor J.B. Bhattacharjee for the Tripura *State Formation in Medieval Tripura* (1982).[38] The formation of the Tripuri State was completed in the fifteenth century. While the pre fifteenth century stage of formation has elements of primary state formation the state or the principality which was built up by Ratna Fa with the help of the Sultan of Gaur is a classical example of secondary state. Other factors are like the Brahmanical influences in the court of Tripura, sanskritisation of the Bodos and their ruling elites including the king, the social stratification, the military organization, the revenue from the plains and gifts and tributes from the tribes, strengthened the Tripura monarchy.

Bhattacharjee's study reveals the elevation of the Tripura political system from a tribal base to a well developed monarchy. The leadership of the tribe passed into a single personality of a hereditary line. During their migrations, they resorted to both shifting cultivation and wet rice cultivation in the plains which were inhabited by the Indo-Aryan migrants. Their exposure to Bengali Hindu influence resulted in social stratification and legitimization of the state of the Chief. The military support from Bengal strengthened the monarch. Bhattacharjee concludes, "The protective position of the ruler and his universalized social status helped him in organizing an elaborate hierarchical order suitable in sustaining the structure and in planting artisans and professionals from other territories without any opposition from the members of the tribe or indigenous population. The support and loyalty of the more productive non tribals were enforced by the Raja's projected role as the champion of his new faith and their cultural and linguistic assimilation with the majority group in the state. The sustenance came in the form of surplus extracting in terms of tribute and taxes and personal service and the Rajas themselves indulging in profitable trades."[39]

J.B. Ganguly, in Economic content of State Formation process in Medieval Tripura (1985) tries to give the economic dimension on the Marxian frame built up by Engels to the emergence of state in Tripura on the basis of changing mode of production which is further elaborated by Samir Amin's four categories of pre-capitalist modes of production, namely,

(i) the primitive-communal, (ii) the tribute paying, (iii) the slave owning, (iv) the simple petty commodity.[40] Ganguly tries to fit the pre-state village level polity structures of the tribals of Tripura in the above frame. According to Ganguly, no state emerged so long the tribes were exclusively engaged in shifting cultivation which did not produce any surplus. Ganguly's study reinforced Bhattacharjee's findings, Ganguly thinks that only after the emergence of private property, the state emerged in Tripura. He concludes, "The process (of settlement of non-tribals and building of as administrative machinery) led to the strengthening of the private ownership of property, restrictions on free access of the tribals to forests and other resources, extension of areas under wet rice cultivation, monetization of productive activities and exchange, usury and collection of land revenue, taxes on commodities and duties on export and import of goods, thus marking the breaking of the gentile constitution (of Engels) and the transition from the primitive communal to the tribute paying mode of production." [41]

**The Ahom state**

The study on Tai Ahoms who were a branch of Mau Shans of Upper Assam engaged the attention of very well known scholars of different disciplines. Amalendu Guha in his very analytical paper, Ahom Political System (1983) examined the process of formation of the Ahom State with a Marxian conceptual frame and methodology. Guha's is not only "a historical study of the evolution of the Ahom social political system, but also a theoretical contribution which discusses a number of issues arising within Engel's problematic as such is of intertest to every student of Marxism" (Editorial comment of Social Scientist). Guha suggests that the formation of the states of Assam, Jaintia, Cachar, Tripura and Manipur should be studied by the students of history and social anthropology. He writes "to any study of the transition from tribalism to statehood, both history and social anthropology can contribute: the former by examining extant records and recorded oral tradition and the latter by sentinizing the fossilised traces of the process which are still within the tribal social structures."[42] After examining Morgan's and Engels' theoretical formulation, Guha observes that statehood emerged only when a community could produce a surplus sufficient for the maintenance of a non-producing public authority. He continues "Smaller the surplus, less elaborate was its public authority structure. In north east India, tribal state formation, early or medieval were made possible by the generation of the requisite surplus from either their own or other people's wet rice cultivation. Rain fed or irrigated, such wet rice farming was again technically made possible by the use of cattle powered plough that ensured a relatively large surplus and, therefore, also a higher form of political organization. Larger the surplus, more developed was the state"[43] With all the historical data with which he is well acquainted, Guha examines the formation of the Ahom state in Assam.[44] He compares the Ahom State formation to the Roman State formation of Engels. The Ahom state is an example of the secondary state formation but Guha reveals the indigenous processes which are inherent in a pristine state formation also. He describes the Ahom Tai social formation at the time of their invasion cum migration to Brahmaputra valley as Marching Peasant commune which was a miniature replica of Tai polity of Burma created a full fledged state in the end of the fourteenth century. Conquest, control over agricultural resources and adoption of wet rice cultivation, social stratification and sanskritization and adoption of language and religion of the majority conquered people have led to the evolution of the full Ahom State. Guha's contribution has become a model for study of state formation in the region.

**R. Buragohain in Tai Ahom state formation**

Role of Conquest and Irrigation in the Origin of the Tai

Ahom States, by Buragohain makes a comprehensive survey of existing theories on conquest and hydraulic culture and finds that only conquest or irrigation alone may not be the cause of the formation of a state. But his study shows that the "Ahom state was a conquest state as they were both invading migrants, hence it was a secondary state. And irrigation provided the infrastructure for social stability in an agraian society engaged in wet rice cultivation."[45] Burgohain in another paper, points out the role of Myth in the Tai Ahom Formation.

## The Khasi states

The Khasi states including the kingdom of Jaintia were at various level of evolution to full fledged state. The Khasi Syiemship is an important field of enquiry for the subject. The kingdom of Jaintia was the most developed of the Khasi Polity formation. Hamlet Bareh in his' The History and Culture of Khasi People' and B. Pakem's study in the Jaintia state formation in S.C. Sinha's workshop are the main study of the subject. B. Pakem's analysis is made with a contemporaneous methodology and scientific treatment.[46]

## The Meitei state

The formation of Meitei state in the fifteenth century after a long period of interclan and inter-societal conflicts among the clan principalities of Manipur valley is a glaring case of the primary state formation. T.C. Hodson, in his *The Meitheis* (1908) gives a broad frame of the Meitei kingdom which was further elaborated in Nandallal Sharma, *Meitrabak* (1960) and N. Ibobi Singh, *Manipur Administration* 1709-1907. Arambam Lokendra's *Manipur, A Ritual Theatre State* (Coronation Model and Concept of Welfare in Meitei Ethno-state system) 1986, examines the Meitei State structure within the framework of the "Theatre structure within the framework of the "Theatre state" developed by Clifford Geartz which denotes "the nature of maintaining political organisation through an integrated pattern of ritual relationship between the centre of power and its subordinate areas."[47] Lokendra points out that the Meitie state was formed out of the "Proto historic fusion of seven cognate clan principalities spread over the wet agriculture areas of the valley." As the title suggests Lokendra's paper is not actually a study in state formation but it analyses within a well thought out frame, the Meitei concept of state, its nature and objective linked up with concept of the welfare. The structure of the Meitei Ethno state was based on Meitei physiological organism. This paper gives a better understanding and insight into the state system of the Meiteis which is necessary to trace out the process of formation of the Meitei state, Lokendra's perceptive paper is an original contribution to Meitei state system and Meitei historiography. For the study of the Meitei state formation, all the existing models ranging from Myth to Marxian system can be applied to ascertain the process of the Meitei state formation.

## Non-state segmentary social structure

Large number of anthropological writings on the tribes have provided ideas of the tribal polity formation. However, M. Horam's Naga Polity is a first study on the pre-state structure of a few selected Naga tribes: the Angami, the Aos and the Tangkhuls T.T. Ao's study of the tabooed chiefs of the Konyaks in his brief note, the Angh of Konyak Naga Society explains the institution of the Chief known as the Angh.[48] Chiefship of the Konyak Nagas is an interesting" instance of pre-state segmentary structure which was created due to the stratification of the Konyak society into four classes; Wangham (great Angh), Wangsa (Samall Angh), Wangsu (intermediate) and Wangpun (Commoners). It is to be established whether the Konyak society is a ranked society or stratified society. The Konyaks are divided into two phratries, Thenkoh and Thendu. The Anghs of these two groups differ in their power and function. The Angh of the Konyak is a religious and political chief with judicial power and controlling power over land resources. The privileges of the Angh like the Kuki chiefs are many; they are of course, more in the form of homage or gifts. Angship should be studied further so that this intermediate structure will help us in understanding the whole process of state formation, Parul Datta's chieftainship among the Nocte and Wanchos of Tirap is a good study.[49]

I would like to end my long survey with a brief reference to the Koch principality and to the Morans of Dibrugarh District of Assam which were studied respectively by J.B. Bhattacharjee[50] and S. Dutta.[51] In the Moran state formation, S. Dutta points out that the Morans are a group of Bodos who migrated to their present habitat in the first millenium B.C. They were shifting cultivators who took to wet rice agriculture by using plough and yoke. Their surplus production led to trade and payment of taxes to the chief who became wealthy and wielded political power. The Moran chiefdom was a pre-state structure. They came into contact with the Ahoms whose suzerainty they accepted. After several centuries, the Moran principality was built up and in 1805 their sovereign status was recognised by the Ahom but they were annexed into British empire in 1839.

## REFERENCES


1. See, Frederick M. Watkin, *International Encyclopedia of Social Sciences,* Vol. 15, p. 150..
2. Henry J.M. Claessen and Peter Skalnik (ed), *Early State,* 1978, The Hague, p. 4.
3. Elman R. Service, *Origin of the State and Civilization: The Process of Cultural Evolutioin,* 1975, New York.
4. ibid.
5. Service op cit., p. 34
6. F Engels, *Origin of Family, Private Property and State* Selected works of Marx and Engels. vol. 3. Progress Publishers, Moscow, 1977, pp. 326-327.

7. V. I. Lenin, *State and Revolution*, Progress Publishers, Moscow, 1977.

8. Engels, op cit., PP 327-328.

9. Ronald Cohen, "State Foundation: A Controlled Comparison" in R. Cohen and E. R. Service (Ed), *Origin of State: The Anthropoligy of Political Evolution*, 1978, Philadelphia, p. 14.

10. Morton H.Fried, "The Chicken and the Egg, or What came First" in Cohen and Service (ed), *Origin of State*, 1978 Philadelphia.

11. Morton H. Freied, *Evolution of Political Society*, 1967. New York.

12. Cohen and Service (Ed). *Origin of State*.

13. Amalendu Guha, "Ahom Political System: An Enquiry into the State Formation Process in Medieval Assam (1228-1714)", *Social Scientist*, December 1983, p.4.

14. ibid

15. Barbara Price, in Cohen and Service, op. cit., p. 161.

16. R. Cohen, "State Foundation: A Controlled Comparison" in Cohen and Service (ed), *Origin of State*, p. 153.

17. See, V. Gordon Childe, *What Happened in History?* 1950, New York. His theory of Urban revolution as the beginning of State has been rejected by many anthropoligists.

18. Barbara Price, op. cit., p. 162.

19. Samir Amin, *Unequal Development*, 1979, Oxford.

20. E. R. Service, *The Origin of State and Civilization: The Process of Cultural Evolution*, 1975, New Yoik, p. 2.

21. Classen and Skalnik, *The Early State*, 1978.

22. See, also the special issue on *State Formation in International Social Science Journal*, 1980, Paris, Vol. XXXII No. 4, particularly the articles of Maurice Godelier and Romila Thapar; Maurice Godelier, Perspectives in Marxist Anthropology, Cambridege, 1977.

23. Romia Thapar, *From Lineage to State*, 1984, Bombay, Oxford University Press, p. 1.

24. ibid.

25. *Man in India*, Vol. 42, No.1. 1962.

26. J.B. Bhattacharjee, "State Fonnation in Precolonial Tribal Norrth East: A Case Study of the Dimasa State", *NEHU Journal of Social Sciences and Humanities*, Vol. II, No.3, 1984, p. 1.
27 K.S. Singh, "State Fonnation in Tribal Society: Preliminary Observation". *Journal of Indian Anthropological Society*, Vol. 6. No.2, October, 1972.
28 K.S. Singh, "A Study in State Formation Among Tribal Communities", *Indian Historical Review*, Indian Council of Historical Research, 1974.
29 Cited by J.B. Bhattacharjee, oP. cit., p. 1.
30 Cited by Romila Thapar, op. cit., p. 4.
31. B. Stein, *Peasant State and Society in Medieval South India*, 1980, Delhi.
32. S.C. Sinha, *The Tribal Polities and State System in Precolonial Eastern and North Eastern India*, Calcutta, 1987.
33. Romila Thapar, op. cit., p. 19.
34. J.B. Bhattacharjee, p. 2.
35. A. Guha, "Ahom Political System", *Social Scientist*, December 1983, P. 4.
36. Maretina in Claessen and Skalnik (ed), *The Early State*.
37. J.B. Bhattacharjee, "State Fonnation in Precolonial tribal North East: A Case study of the Dimasa State", *NEHU Journal of Social Sciences and Humanities*, Vol. 11, No. 3, 1984, pp. 3-4.
38. J.B. Bhattacharjee, "Tripuri State Fonnation in Medieval Tripura", *Proceedings of the Third Session of the North East India History Asscociation*, 1982.
39. J.B; Bhattacharjee, op. cit., p. 72.
40. J.B. Ganguly, "Economic Content of State Fonnation Process in Medieval Tripur", *Proceedings of the Sixth Session of North East India History Association*, 1985, pp. 146-159.
41. J.B. Ganguly, op. cit., p. 159.
42. A Guha, "The Ahom Political System: An Enquiry into the State Formation Process in Medieval Assam (1228-1714)", Social Scientists, December, 1983, p.1.
43. A Guha, op. cit., p. 41

44. See, his earlier works especially, "Tribalism to Feudalism in Asaam *1600-1750", Indian Historical Research*, Vol. 1. 1974.
45. R. Buragohain, "Tai-Ahom State Fonnation: Role of Conquest and Irrigation in the Origin of the Tai Ahom State," *Proceedings of the Fifth Session of the North East India History Association*, 1984.
46. H. Bareh, *History and Culture of Khasi People;* B. Pakem, "Jaintia State Fonnation" in S.C. Sinha (Ed), *Tribal Polities and State Systems in Eastern and North Eastern India.*
47. Lokendra Arambam, A Ritual Theatre State ('Coronation model and concept of welfare in Metei ehtno state system'), *Manipur University Research Journal*, Humanities and Social Sciences, Vol. III, No. 1,1986, pp. 31- 47.
48. T.T. Ao, "The Ang of Konyak Nagas", *Proceedings of the Second Session of the North East India History Association*, 1981.
49. Parul Dutta, "The Institution of Chieftainship among the Nokte and Wancho of Tirap District of Arunachal Pradesh", *Proceedings of the Second Session of the North East India History Association*, 1981.
50. J.B. Bhattacharjee, "The Koch Principality in Cachar", *Proceedings of the Second Session of the North East India History Association*, 1981.
51. S. Dutta, "The Moran State Fonnation in Asaam", *Proceedings of the Fifth Session of the North East India History Association*, 1984.

CHAPTER ELEVEN

# HISTORY WRITING IN MANIPUR

The people of Manipur have a strong historical sense. With the art of writing developed at a very early stage of the Meitei civilization, the record keeping or chronicle keeping was started in the fifteenth century. But there are literary texts dealing with historical events which were written in the early period, (as claimed by the writers,) around the beginning of the Christian era. Education and scholarship were controlled by the royalty and nobility and this had limited to a very few scholars patronized and utilized by the monarch. The king-controlled-writing was reflected in chronicle keeping. The Meitei view of the past (or history) was holistic approach; naturally it was difficult to separate what was historical from what was myth, legends and tradition, and from religion and theology. History writing was dominated by the interest or consideration of the royalty and theology. The classic example is *Leithak Leikharon* an eighteenth century text which was a compendium of cosmology, genealogy, myth and legends, culture and religion; statecraft and history, which a typical educated Meitei Scholar or Maichow was expected to have a full knowledge. A Maichow was a scholar, a priest, an astrologer and advisor to the royalty or nobility. Practical necessity required the Maichows to look at society, state and religion as a whole, and their knowledge became a generalized and comprehensive one, or with some great scholars, encyclopaedic. Historical particularism or special differentiation of history did not develop in the ancient and medieval period.

Records, chronicles, or puyas were not only "historical pieces" but they were used a manuals for administration. Religious performance, social and judicial dispensation and culture affairs. Perhaps it was due to this reason that history as a distinct and separate branch of knowledge did not develop in ancient Manipur. And the philosophy of history of the ancient Meitei was to know the past, use the knowledge of the past for the present needs; and the action and achievement of the past should be kept for the knowledge of the posterity. The king and the nobility had a strong concern for the "Posterity". Further, they should know what was achieved by the monarchs in the past for the perpetuation of their fame. We find, therefore, a sense of the past, greatly influenced by the need of the present and by a desire for glorification by the posterity. Hence, the great concern for control over event recording chronicles.

The tribals in the hills were also greatly concerned with their past preserved through oral tradition, genealogy and folklore. The tribal account of their past, narrated or preserved in mythical form are believed to be authentic by themselves. The Nagas have their history in folklore, hymns and songs and migration accounts. The Kuki tribes keep their authentic genealogy for generations and centuries even as thorough as possible. The genealogical trees or accounts are the backbone of their past. In the pre modern period, among the tribals, the Marings appear to be the most learned group. The knowledge of writing with the Meitei script was known to the select Maring scholars. For other tribes, modern education was a product of the colonial period and a gift of Christianity. Conversion to Christianity and contact with the British rule were the landmarks of the tribal social development or historical development.

The "consciousness" of history became very much pronounced in Manipur with the sanskritization of the Meitei royalty and populace in the eighteenth century. The writing of history, keeping of chronicles, use of eras and calendars, origin of the ruling dynasty, the people and country were sanskritized. Religious conversion and resultant perception of the Hinduised or Aryan identity had influenced history writing in Manipur since the Hinduization of Manipur. But modern history writing as such was a contribution of the colonial ethnographers and administrators who were posted in Manipur.

King Garibaniwaz, the great Hinduised ruler of Manipur caused a history of Manipur called *Vijoy Panchali* to be "written in 1730 A.D. based on a sanskritized royal genealogy of the Ningthouja dynasty. There are references to Manipur in the writing of the British officers in the 18th century and early 19th century.

J.P. Wade, an English surgeon who accompanied Captain Welsh in his expedition to Assam in 1792-94 mentions the Mughal or Mussalman connection with Manipur in his *Account of Assam*. Francis Hamilton in his *Account of Assam* (1808) devotes a section on Manipur. With the Burmese conquest of Manipur known as the Seven Year Devastation (1819-26) and consequent involvement of Manipur in the first Anglo-Burmese war and posting of British military officers of the East India Company, there grew up an active interest among the officers in the history, ethnography of Manipur and her inhabitants both the Meiteis and the hill tribes. Mention may be made of Francis Jenkins who became a commissioner of Assam, George Gordon the first political agent in Manipur and R.B. Pemberton, who as a young subaltern volunteered to join the small guerilla force of Gambhir Singh, the exiled prince of Manipur in his historic liberation movement to drive away the Burmese from his kingdom and who later on represented

Manipur as a commissioner in the great Kabaw Valley dispute with Burma may be regarded as the pioneer of modem historical researches in Manipur. His Report on the *North Eastern Frontier of British India* was published in 1835 with a major portion devoted to Manipur. Pemberton's Report, as it came to be popularly known, has been a reference work not only on Manipur but on all adjoining areas of India and Burma including the kingdom of Pong. He studied the extant chronicles and available historical literatures and in course of his research, he discussed a Pong Chronicle (a chronicle of Shan kingdom of Mogaung) which refers to the invasion of Manipur by Shans in the eight century and conquest of Kabaw valley by Manipur. He rejected the Hindu origin of the Meiteis and propounded an untenable theory of Tartar origin of the same people. His knowledge of the history of Manipur covers the eighteenth and early nineteenth centuries. Two years later, George Gordon published a dictionary of English and Manipuri in 1837. *A note on Thadou Grammar* by Sopitt was published in 1857. W. McCulloch who served twenty three years in Mainipur, a man of culture and literary ability published his *Account of the Valley of Manipore and surrounding hill tribes* in 1859. His knowledge of history as found in the Account has not increased much since Pemberton; but his observations on ethnography, economy and culture of Manipur, are highly accurate and the work remains for many decades, a chief authority on the subject. His reference to early history before in 18th Century contains Manipur-Pong connection since the 8th century. He perhaps studied the old chronicles of the kingdom. E.T. Dalton's *Descriptive Ethnology of Bengal* (1872) contains some accounts of Manipur tribes. McClloch was succeeded by R. Brown, a surgeon as political agent who published his *Statistical Account of Manipur* in 1874 which is an important study on history and culture of the people of the state. One philogogist who would have contributed a lot to the knowledge of Manipur and north east India was G.H. Damant of the Indian Civil Service but his untimely death in 1879 at Khonoma in Nagaland. He was for some time officiating Political agent in Manipur and published research papers on Manipur in the journals of *Asiatic Society of Bengal and Royal Asiatic Society.*

But the history of Manipur in the proper sense was not attempted till Alexander Mackenzie's celebrated *History of the Relation of the Government with hill tribes of North Eastern Frontier of British Bengal* which was published in 1884. Manipur being outside the British India empire, occupies a place of pride in this work. This book represents the official views of historical events and is regarded as "authentic" history based on official records of the Government ofIndia. E. W. Dun's *Gazetteer of Manipur,* 1886 and its abridged edition, 1891 were publish. In 1890, perhaps against the writing of the British writers, rejecting Manipur's Aryan origin, the first history of Manipur in Manipuri was published by Haodeijamba Cheitanya. His *Manipur Itihas* gives the dynastic history of Manipur based on the chronicles written after Hinduisation. The British conquest of Manipur in 1891 and the controversial action of the British officers including Chief Commissioner F.J. Quinton and Political Agent Grimwood and the behaviour of the king and princes of Manipur created fresh interest on Manipur. *My Three Years in Manipur* by Mrs. Ethel Grimwood, 1891 gave a personal account of the events. The Indian view was presented in RG. Basak's *Manipur Prahalika,* 1891 in Bengali and Manmohan Ghosh's *Did the Manipuri Princes get affair Trial?*, 1891 containing the legal documents. These works are not history but eyewitness accounts and documents of the last days of Manipur's independent existence. There was a lot of criticism over Manipur affairs after the War and James Johnstone, a former Political Agent who had a distinguished career as a frontier officer in India published his *My Experience in Manipur and Naga Hills* in 1896. These works are not an important contribution to scientific ethnography but Johnstone's work gives interesting information on the character of the people and some historical accounts. Ghosh's and Basak's works are important sources of history of the events. After the conquest, encouragement was given for the translation of the chronicles which was well utilised by ethnographers like T.C. Hodson and John Shakespeare in early twentieth century, the interest on Manipur was encouraged, B.C. Allen's *Gazetteer of Naga Hills and Manipur* 1904 was the first of the several remarkable works. Then came T.C. Hodson's *Magnum Opus,* the *Meitheis* in 1908. Hodson was an Assistant Political Agent in Manipur whose services was terminated for having shot dead a tribal porter; he later joined the University of London. He was the first scholar with anthropological knowledge to have studied the Meiteis and the Naga and Kuki tribes. Hodson's *Meitheis* is still the best full scale study of the Meiteis, their society, polity, religion, and culture based on the ethnological and historical evidences. His *Naga Tribes of Manipur,* 1911 is the first comprehensive work on the Nagas of Manipur but it is not as remarkable as the first work. Another frontier officer who did a lot for the ethnography, and folklore of Manipur and Mizoram was John Shakespeare. His *Lushai-Kuki Clans,* 1913 is still a very authentic work on the subject. Shakespeare contributed well written papers on religious beliefs of the Meiteis in learned journals. On the language front G.A Grierson's monumental work, *Linguistic Survey of India* Vol. III part II and III deal with the languages and dialects of different tribes and communities of Manipur, Meitei, Naga and Kuki. Mention may be made of William Pettigrew's *Tangkhul Grammar* which is a first authentic study on the Tangkhuls. Another exciting discovery during the period was G.R Gerini's *Research on Ptolemy's Geography,* 1909 which, refers to the existence of a Hindu kingdom in Manipur in the 6th century B.C. based on a Burmese Chronicle. *Manipur Purabritta* the second work on history of Manipur by a local writer, written by P. Parijat was published in 1917.

He gave the genealogy of the rulers with their chronology. He proposed that Nongda Lairen Pakhangba might have ruled in the fourth century AD. and not form 33 AD.

Shakespeare's interest also influenced other capable officers to write on the tribes of Manipur like, Christopher Gimson's *Notes on Maring Nagas,* William Shaws's *Notes on Thadou Kukis.* Abdul Ali the Indian archivist published his *Note on Early History of Manipur* in 1923 which deals with early Manipur's contact with the East India Company. Inspite of some deficiencies, this small work was important and significant information about 18th century Manipur work was important and significant information about 18th century Manipur which has been well used by later historians. L. W. Shakespeare's *History of Assam Rifles,* 1929 deals with the exploits of the Assam Rifles, a para-military forces who acted as the sentinel of the eastern frontier, in Manipur in the War of 1891 and Kuki Rebellion of 1917-19.

Sanskrit and English educated scholars of Manipur had started writing on history of Manipur. Among them Panditraj Atombapu Sharma and W. Yumjao Singh were the foremost; the former represented the literary school and the latter represented the historical school. Panditraj Atombapu (1889-1963) wrote more than one hundred papers and books. His first wellknown book was *Haree Mayee* (translated into English by Arambam Dorendro Singh) which was reviewed by J.C. Higgins of Indian Civil Service. It deals with the Vedic interpretation of the origin and history of Manipur. His *Manipur Itihas* was published in 1940. *Pakhangba* was published in 1953. W. Yumjao Singh was an amateur archeologist, his *Report on the Archaeological Studies* in Bulletin No.1. 1935 is a landmark in the historical stu lies in the state. His discovery of coins of the second century A.D. and the controversial Phayeng Plates added a new dimension to the history of Manipur. His later works, *Manipur Itihas,* 1946, and *Early History of Manipur* (1966), published posthumously do not have the earlier historical touch. Khumanthem Kaomacha's *Manipur Itiibritti,* 1938 is an improved account of history of Manipur so far attempted. He listed the names of books alleged to have been burnt during the reign of Garibaniwaz under the instruction of a fanatic Hindu missionary. The fact that these books were well remembered at a period of conservative Hindu heyday in Manipur shows that the copies of these books were available. Mutum Jhulon's *Vijoy Panchali* in English is a commendable work, though it was not highly scientific work.

Robert Reid, a Governor of Assam in continuation of the tradition of Mackenzie, published his *History of Areas Bordering Assam* in 1942 devoting a chapter on Manipur, coming of the Anglo-Manipur War and colonial rule in Manipur. One should remember the pioneering work of R.K. Sanahal Singh, *Manipur Itihas,* 1947. This is a short but well documented work.

Since Abdul Ali, Manipur did not receive much attention of Indian scholars, though some references to her were made in the works dealing with the British Burma War, A.C. Bannerjee's *British Annexation of Burma,* RM. Lahiri, *Annexation of Assam,* S.K. *BhuyanAnglo-Assamese Relation* give some references to Manipur. However, S.K. Chatterjee, a friend of Manipur and Manipuri literature devotes a sizable section on early history, language and culture of Manipur in his *Kirata Jana Kriti* published in 1950. J.Roy's *A*

*History of Manipur* 1958 was first of its kind in English. This work is factual and refreshing, in comparison with the monotony of the earlier works. Interest in Manipur's history was always aroused in the British conquest of Manipur, RC. Majumdar's *War against Manipur,* 1955. Small works but handy like, H.Bijoy Singh, *Meitrabakki Wari,* Nandalal Sharma's *Meitrabak* (1960), L.M.Iboongohal Singh's *An Introduction of Manipur* (1960 and 1963) came out. Nandalal Sharma's Meitrabak is still an important work of reference next to Hodson's *The Meitheis,* RK. Jhalajit Singh, *A Short History of Manipur* (1965) is history of the Ningthouja dynasty of Manipur based on indigenous sources which had not been utilised so far. This is an improvement on J.Roy's history. This book was built up around the royal chronicle *Cheitharol Kumbaba* in early period and from other sources in the later periods. In the 1960's there was strong awareness of need for historical writings. The publication of old chronicles and historical literatures was taken up by research organisations and individual scholars who were given financial assistance by the state. The *Cheitharol Kumbaba,* the royal chronicle of Manipur was edited by L.M. Iboongohal Singh and N. Khelchandra Singh and published by the Manipuri Sahitya Parishad in 1967. O. Bhogeswar Singh published *Ningthourol Lambuba,* another Chronicle without chronology in 1968. Many old historical works in Manipur were published Y. Bheigya's *Leithak Leikharon,* N. Khelchandra's *Chada Laihui, Naothingkhong Phambal Kaba., Khumanlol,* genealogy of the Khuman, O. Bhogeswar's *Ningthourol Sheireng,* 1967 Khumanlamba Yaima's *Pakhangba Phambal* (coronation of Pakhangba) 1967, *Poireiton Khunthokpa* (colonization of Poi rei ton, 1969). Works in Manipuri like L. Chandramani Singh's *Manipur Itihas* which deals with Anglo-Manipuri relation upto 1891 came out in 1970. W. Gourchandra's *Manipurigi Aroiba Lal* (War of 1891) RK. Sanahal's *Chingthangkhomba Ganga Chatpa* (Bheigyachandra's pilgrimage to Bengal), *Bir Tikendrajit Singh, Thangal General*, N. *Khelchandra'sAriba Manipuri Sahityagi Itihas* (1969) were published. Other works are O. Bhogeswar's *Sanamahi Laikan* (1973), Chandrasekhar's *Loiyamba Shilyen* (Royal Decree of Loiyumba) N. Ibochouba's *Thiren Laiyat* (a text on Meitei Philosophy), O. Bhogeswor's *Kangbalon* (Chronicle of Kangba), *Shakok Lamlen* (a work on Meitei religious belief). The *Vijoy Panchali*, in four volumes written originally by Kritichandra in Bengali was translated into Manipuri by Mani Singh and Mangi Singh in 1966. S.N. Parratt, *Religion of Manipur*, Lal Dena's *British Policy towards Manipur* are good research works. Several research journals both in English and Manipur deal with different aspects of the history and culture of Manipur. Both institutional and individual researches are still continuing. Institutions like, the Manipur Sahitya Parishad, Manipur University (Erstwhile Jawaharlal Nehru University Post-Graduate Centre) Manipur State Kala Akademi, Manipur State Museum, Manipur State Archive, State Archaeology Department and Mutua Museum have contributed greatly to the growth of historical studies.

For pre-history and proto-history, the archaeological excavations carried out by O.K. Singh of Archaeology Dept. in **Kangkhui Cave** (Ukhrul), **Tharon Cave** (Tamenglong) and **Napachink** (Wangoo) are revealing many new data and collection of inscription, sculptures, coins, other evidences are going on. Mutua Museum's Collection of coins is breaking new grounds in numismatic studies. The bulletins of the Museum and P. Gunindro's *Manipuri Numismatics* (1983) are commendable works. On the cultural and ethnographic studies, we may mention, the *Ritual Dances of Manipur* by Lightfoot, *Aspects of Indian Culture* by E. Nilakanta, K.B. Singh (ed.) *An introduction to Tribal Language and Culture*, M. Horam's *Naga Polity and Socio-culturallife of the Nagas* (Tangkhul). Asoso

Yuno's *Naga Struggle. against the British under Jadonang and Gaidinliu,* Gangmumei Kabui's *Anal- Transborder Tribe of Manipur,* M Chaki-Sarkar's *Feminism in Traditional Society: Women of Manipur Valley.* W. Ibohal Singh's *A History of Manipur Early Period* (1986).

Sanajaoba Naoria edited *Manipur: Past and Present* in three volumes is an excellent compendium on various aspects of history, society polity, and culture of Manipur. It is a great contribution made by Sanajaoba Naoria. The three volumes with documents like chronicles, treaties and constitutional extracts have becom : a good reference work on anything concerning Manipur, Gangmumei Kabui's *History of Manipur in the pre-colonial Period* (1991) in a definitive history of ancient and medieval Manipur based on a clear cut historical methodology. This is a critical study of the evolution of the kingdom of Manipur with emphasis on state formation process. It reflects the latest trend in historiography of Manipur. It is a fresh and rational study of the history of Manipur free from bias and prejudices.

N. Joykumar's *Social Movements in Manipur* (1919-1950) is a pioneer work on the Social movements, both theoretical and empirical. It is definitely a great contribution to modern history of Manipur. Lal Dena's edited *Modern History of Manipur* 1826-1949 is a collection learned papers by Gangmumei Kamei, Lal Dena and N. Joykumar on different aspects of modern history of Manipur.

John and Saroj N. Parratt's *Queen Empress Vs Prince Tikendrajit of Manipur* is a historical narrative based on archive and press reports. It uses hitherto unutilized source materials of British museum and other, while the narrative in flowery style is excellent, authors are not clear about the nature of the conflict between Manipur and the British which was a war between Manipur and the British. India presided over by Queen Empress Victoria and independent Manipur. The authors avoided using the term "War" and confine themselves to using the term "conflict" only. However, Pandit N. Khelchandra Singh "Documents of the Anglo Manipurwas of 1891" in two volumes is a very useful work both for the scholars and common people. This is a great service rendered by the great pandit towards the histriography of the British conquest of Manipur, 1891.

*The Lost Kingdom*, an English translation of the Cheitharol Kumbaba made by a Bengali clerk of the office of the Political Agency in Manipur was located by L. Joychandra Singh in the India office Library London and he published it with some good photographs. *The Lost Kingdom* is the first English version of the celebrated Cheitharol Kumbaba, the royal chronicle of Manipur. Contemporary historical research was focused on the Merger of Manipur into India (1949) and the Revolt of Hijam Irabot Singh, 1948-1951. We may mention H. Bhubhan Singh's *Merger of Manipur* and the "Annexation of Manipur" on a 'collection of the papers on the *National Convention on Merger* (1943). These two works reflect contemporary assessment of Merger and its implications. K. Manimohon Singh's H. *Irabot Singh and his political Movement* is a full scale study on the great revolutionary leader of modem Manipur. There are a large number of books and papers on the great leader of Manipur.

Recently, the History department of Manipur University, Manipur History society, State Archive and State Archaeology have been doing yeoman service to history writing in Manipur.

**The Cheitharol Kumbaba**

The celebrated Cheitharol Kumbaba is the most important royal chronicle of Manipur which records the historical events of nearly two thousand years covering the reign of 78 kings from Nongda Lairen Pakhangba (33-154A.D.) to Bodh Chandra Singh (1941-55). The unique chronicle written in Meitei script is kept in the royal palace and entry to this state diary is made by the learned royal scribes. Even now, this tradition of history keeping is still continued by the **Pandit Loisang,** the college of priests in the royal palace of Manipur. This chronicle was written out in Bengali script and edited by Pandit Thongam Madhob Singh and published by Visvabharati Mandir. Then with the permission granted by Maharaja Churachand Singh, the chronicle was edited by L.M. Iboongohal Singh and N. Khelchandra Singh and published by the Manipur Sahitya parishad in 1967.

The Cheitharol Kumbaba has three phases; the early phase from Nongda Lairen Pakhangba to 1484 A.D. during the reign of Kyamba, the middle phase from 1484 A.D. to 1780 A.D. During the reign of Bheigyachandra and the later phase from 1780 A.D. to the middle of twentieth century. Cheitharol Kumbaba is a combination of two practices; Cheitharol comes from the word Cheithaba which was established in 1484 A.D. by king Kyamba, to substitute the announcement of the end of the year by a stick holding person known as **Cheithaba.** Cheithaba means giving up of the stick expressing the end of the year.

Cheithaba is also a state ceremony of making a person a scapegoat for the evil burdens of the king and the country for the coming year. The person is called Cheithaba of the year and the year is named after him. He is given tax free land and other privileges like exemption from feudal dues. The first Cheithaba in 1484 A.D. was Hiyangloi. Kumbaba or Kumpaba means counting of years, (kum = year: paba = counting). Thus Cheitharol Kumbaba means counting of years according to Cheithaba.

The chronicle keeping was started from this year 1484. A.D. the year of Hiyangloi, the Cheithaba. Therefore, the early phase of this Chronicle which deals with the pre-Kyamba rulers is extremely sketchy. It was definitely a later recording reconstructed out of the available sources of informations. From Nongda Lairen Pakhangba to Kiyamba, there are 38 kings and they are historical personalities. The Hindu mythical rulers given in the chronicles above Pakhangba were later interpolations. Though sketchy, these events are quite historical and corroborated by other chronicles. So it would be clear that this was reconstructed by the writers of the Chronicle. The year of the accession and end of the rule of a particular king was mentioned.

The middle phase from 1484 to 1780 A.D. from Kyamba to Bheigyachandra, it has become quite reliable. The year and month of the events are mentioned. Later on even the dates and days are also mentioned. But due to the repeated Burmese invasions of Manipur in the second half of the eighteenth century, the chronicle was lost. And it was rewritten in 1780 A.D. at the palace of Kanchipur at the order of King Bheigyachandra, by Chirom Shyarnram and Oinam Anandaram under the supervision of the uncle of the king, Ananta Shai Khwairakpa. This is recorded in the chronicle itself. The impact of the rewriting is reflected in the entries of the events before this date with regard to the record of birth of princes, accession to the throne and death of kings. For instance, the Chronicle records that king Khagemba was born in 1576 A.D. And king Charairongba was born in 1637 A.D. At the time of their birth they were princes, sons of their parents, the reigning kings. A son of a king is born as a prince but not born as a king. Therefore, one notices that the contemporaneous recording is not reflected. In the later phase in the post 1780 AD. period, the entries are properly recorded. But again the Burmese occupation of Manipur (1819-26) disrupted the regular keeping of the royal diary. So in 1844, when Nara Singh became the ruler, he ordered the royal astrologer to prepare the Chronicle for the period concerned with the help of six other scholars. Thangchamcha Shyampurna made the actual entries. During the Anglo-Manipur War of 1891 the Chronicle was not entered; so Major Maxwell, the Political Officer of the British occupation force ordered the entry in the Chronicle. The major portion of the Chronicle is devoted to eighteenth, nineteenth and twentieth centuries. The contents of the Chronicle are varied and almost all embracing. Taking at random, the Chronicle records the accession of the ruler on the throne, and death of kings. The year, month, date and day are also mentioned. The military conquest and the military expedition, names of heroes and prisoners of war, description of the actual fighting, weapons used, animals and weapon captured, tribute realised are all recorded. The royal decrees for administrative changes, creation of departments, appointment of nobles to different posts, exemption from state service, the rates of taxes in the form of service and kind are not left out. The royal excursions or pleasure trips to lakes and pilgrimage to abode of deities, tragedies in boat drowning of nobles are not forgotten. The record includes major cultural and social events: The tribal festival in October at the royal palace, invention of drum during the reign of Khuyoi Tampok introduction of particular games like Kaang, Horse Hockey, beginning of a Ratha Jatra, car festival of the Hindu, visits of holy men from India, migration of Brahmin and Muslim to Manipur, writing of books, performance of religious sacrifices and festivals. There are occasions of birth of royal children, death of important personalities, performance of Sati by widows of royalty in early eighteenth century. The punishment of criminals. Exile of penal settlements, religious conversion are also recorded. The fixation of boundaries between Manipur and the Shan kingdom of Pong in 15th century, between Manipur and Burma, and Naga Hills, disputes between Manipur and foreign power are well described. Even capture of leopard and tigers, in the vicinity of the capital, gladiatorial fight between animals and men in the market places, dredging of the river beds are mentioned. The visits of Lord Curzon and Lord Irwin, the Viceroys of India to Manipur are also recorded. Even the royal suspicion of a queen for alleged infidelity of the *king* is found. *This Chronicle is* extremely useful document for the *reconstruction* of all aspects of the *history* of Manipur.

The Cheitharol Kumbaba adopted three chronological systems or eras: Kalyabda, Saka era, Chandrabda or Manipur (Kangleipak) era. The Chronicle opens with accession of Nongda Lairen Pakhangba on the throne in Kalyabda 3135 and *it* records that forty five years after the accession of Pakhangba Sakabda was stated. *Since* Saka era was started *in* 78 AD. Pakhangba's accession was dated 78 AD – 45 = 33 AD. It was due to later interpolation of the entry. The reignal years of the seventy eight rulers from Pakhangba to Bodha Chandra *Singh* were recorded in the Saka era. The adoption of the Sakabda must have been effected after Manipur's conversion to Hinduism. Manipur is well known for her astrologers and astronomers. However during the reign of Bheigyachandra, the Cheitharol Kumbaba adopted two eras :Saka era and Chandrabda. Gambhir *Singh,* a future *king* was recorded to have been born on Wednesday, 28, Phairen, 1709, Sakabda, and 999, Chandrabda. The Chronicle itself records the preparation of calendar and establishment of era called Kangleipak Era which was equated with Chandrabda. By backdating, the Kangleipak or Manipur era or Chandrabda was *fixed* in 788 AD.

With regard to its authenticity, the introductory preface giving mythical rulers as the ancestors of Nongda Lairen Pakhangba are later invention are just ignored. Through the contents of the Chronicle make the rulers from Pakhangba onward historical, the Chronicle says that the first seven kings are divine beings which is not correct as there are various historical evidences to establish their historicity. Those events which are corroborated by other chronicles and independent sources may be accepted as authentic. However, from 13th century onward, the *Chronicle is highly* reliable. Pre-fifteenth century *informations* as noted already are very brief: but a visit of Shan prince Shamlongpha is correctly noted by a *Shan Chronicle*. The chronology before Kyamba was highly doubtful and it is rightly suspected that it is a later addition. So the events described in the chronicle are all antedated.

It will be worthwhile to recall what the pioneer historians said about the Cheitharol Kumbaba. L.M. Iboongohal describes it as the most authoritative diary and history of Manipur and most authentic manuscript. But W. Yumjao Singh expressed doubt about the authenticity of the work. He writes, "Cheitharol Kumbaba a Royal chronicle would have been the most valuable work for historical investigation, as it professes to record all the important daily happenings and occurrences of the state, but here also we are deceived, as there is a passage which clearly says that in the year 1780 A.D. by order of Jai Singh this book was rewritten as the former copy was not available. It is not a matter of joke to recollect things of daily occurrences with their dates. Many of these I think had to be based on hearsay and thus we ha''e to think seriously before we take everything within the book for granted. Another defect of this book is its having been under the strict supervision of the authorities. It does not record any of the particidal and fratricidal incident of the 18th and 19th centuries. But it records the changes of rulers suppressing the historically important movements and information".

We may not agree with Yumjao Singh's charge of deception against the writers of the Chronicle. The important nobles and scholars used to keep private copies of the diary in their private collection and king Jai Singh's scribes might have copied from them. Many modifications and alterations must have been made during the rewriting of the Chronicle. So it may not be most authentic document but is very useful and important document.

The Chronicle deals with the exploits of the Meitei kings and gives a biased view. It also reflects the royalty's view of people and events. The religious conflicts of 18th century are not reflected in the Royal Chronicle. Naturally a historian will accept a source only after a great scrutiny of the material. Despite these deficiencies, the Cheitharol Kumbaba provides information for the reconstruction of the history of Manipur.

## CHAPTER TWELVE

# REINTERPRETATION OF HISTORY
## Ethnic Response To Merger

### Historical Importance of the Reassessment of the Merger Question

The importance of a historical event is judged by the interest shown by the posterity, the historians and in-tellectuals or common people in the form of continuous assessment, critical examination and new interpretation in the light of the felt needs of a nation, country or community. The views of a societal group on the particular historical event also change according to the changing perception of the event on the part of the ruling group or the social groups or the historians. Thus the Merger of Manipur into India in 1949 assumes importance with the changing perception of the question in the mind of the present generation in the light of the present social and political realities and the aspirations of the people. The ongoing reassessment of the Merger question on a massive scale is unprecedented and is of historic importance which will have definite influence in shaping Manipur's relationship with mainland India. It has a great relevance to historiography and nation building process in Manipur. It is a classic example of historical reinterpretation of a historical event.

The Merger was a great landmark and a turning point in the history of Manipur. The Merger was a political decision forced on Manipur through the Maharaj, by the Government of India, to merge into the Dominion of India, in the wake of rising Indian nationalism after India's independence which had an echo in the political life of Manipur in the post merger period.

The purpose of this brief note is to highlight the Government of India's policy, either British or Indian towards the ethnic groups, specially the hill tribes during the post Second World War, their participation in the democratic process in Manipur during the constitutional monarchy and the impact of the Merger on the evolution of the political aspirations of the tribal people and their general attitude towards India and Manipur.

## Two Trends in the Government of India's Policy

The Second World War exposed Manipur and North East India to the outside world with its ravages and suffering caused to the people. There were hopes and aspirations and at the same time fear and apprehensions about the future of the hill people of north east India including Manipur.

The Shillong based political leaders raised the demand of a separate hill state or province for the tribal areas of the region. Kohima based **Naga National Council** demanded independence for the Nagas. The Aizawl based Mizo Union submitted memorandum for integration of Mizo tribes in a single political unit. The ideas and opinions were not popular among the hill tribes or Manipur; though there grew up a number of tribal organisations which aimed at the protection of the tribal interest in the eventual withdrawal of the British from India. Major tribal organisations were the **Kabui Naga Association** (later on Manipur Zeliangrong Union) the Tangkhul Long, the **Kuki National Assembley** (KNA), the **Khuls Union, Gangte Tribal Union, Paite National Union** etc. However, NNC's demand for Naga independence and the Mizo Union's dernand for Mizo integration were not welcomed generally except among some sections like the Hmar and Mao leaders.

There were two elements in the Government of British India's policy. First, they wanted the hill tribes of North East India to exclude themselves from any political arrangements that might be created after independence. They made the proposal for a Crown colony covering hill North East India and upper Burma. At the same time they offered autonomy for the Nagas as indicated in the 9 point agreement between **Naga National Council** and Governor Sir Akbar Hydari of Assam in 1946. Second, in the case of Manipur, they encouraged the establishment of a representative form of government under a Constitutional monarchy. The Maharajah and some leading political leaders including tribal leaders were involved in the introduction of the **Manipur State Constitution Act,** 1947. The British wanted clearly the continuation of the State of Manipur with internal autonomy with treaty relation with India. There was active participation of the tribal educated leaders in the formulation of the democratic institutions in Manipur. Perhaps it was because of this wise policy that the tribal people's attitude towards NNC and Mizo Union was that of indifference.

There were three different trends in the policy of free India's attitude towards hill areas of North East India including Manipur. While Mahatama Gandhi's humanistic liberal approach was for that of non-violence and voluntary participation in the Indian union. Pandit Jawaharlal Nehru's policy was that of paternalism and autonomy for the hill people and for the protection of the political and cultural identity of Manipur within the Indian Union. On Mahatma Gandhi's strong pressure and Pandit Nehru's strong support the safeguards for the tribal and VI Schedule autonomy was provided in Indian Constitution. On the other hand, Sadar Patel's policy was for "integration" of the princely states with Dominion of India, which, in ultimate analysis, as far as north east India is concerned, was the extension of the *"Forward policy"* of the British followed since the 19th century. He was of the opinion that the ethnic background of the region including Manipur was different from that of mainland India and he had deep suspicion of the loyalty of the people. Hence the strong Arm policy of Sadar Patel was carried out by Governor Sri Prakash and Advisor Nari Rustomjee. Paternalism, humanism and autonomy of Gandhi and Nehru were represented by Sir Akbar Hydari. Nehru was not involved and perhaps was not aware of the democratic process and the constitutional monarchy. So Patel had the last say on Manipur affairs. Pandit Nehru, of course made up, when he rejected the recommendation of the States Reorganisation Commission and decided to keep the separate political entity of Manipur as a Union Territory, a status the people of Manipur for obvious reasons did not like.

**Reaction to the Merger: The Tribal Attitude**

For the first time in the long history of struggle for survival from the life of subjugation and oppression under the feudal rule of the monarchy and the British colonialism, the tribal people of Manipur were given the democratic right of franchise for selecting their representatives to the legislature of Manipur under the Manipur State Constitution Act, 1947. They had participated in the new political system under the constitution as MLAs and ministers. There were 18 MLAs from hill areas and two ministers in the council of ministers. The tribal people were grateful to Maharaja Bodh Chandra and his younger brother Chief Minister Maharajakumar Priya Brata Singh for the 'gift of democracy' to them. The tribals who were for centuries neglected and downtrodden were hoping for a new life. They wanted a successful working of the democratic system. There were two opinions among the tribals, one represented by R. Khathing, a 'war hero turned Hill Minister and TC. Tiankham, the speaker of the Assembly; the other represented by A. Daiho, a young leader from Mao who was for assertion of the Naga rights and for independence.

When the agitation for the abolition of monarchy, there were a lot of speculation and misgivings among the tribal leaders about the Government of India's attitude towards the Maharaja vis-a-vis the future of Manipur. T.C. Tiankham, the Speaker of the Assembly expressed his apprehension in a letter to the Maharaja and stressed that the future of Manipur should be decided by. the Assembly which represented the people of Manipur. The Merger came and the tribal leaders were left in a total disarray. They could not and did not react jointly. A. Daiho was against the merger. He was put into jail in connection with the Mao Agitation and was released, later on he became an Advisor to the Chief Commissioner who was assisted by an Advisory Council. R. Kathing, the war hero and the Hill minister went back to civil services in NEFA while TC. Tiankham joined the service of the Government of Manipur.

During the post-merger period, one does not notice any organised ethnic response to it but there were sporadic reactions from the individuals tribal leaders. Then came the all-India political parties; the Congress had achieved their goal for merger with India with great relish. The Socialist (Praja Socialist Party, PSP) demanded further integration of Manipur into the province of Assam. A. Daiho in a memorandum submitted to the States Reorganisation Commission (SRC) made a proposal for a hill state comprising Manipur, Naga Hills and Lushai Hills. Meanwhile, Rishang Keishing, a young M.P. from Outer Manipur (1952) led a sizeable section of the hill people in the agitation for regrant of statehood to manipur.

While his party was for the merger of Manipur *into* Assam, Rishang Keishing personally was for the maintenance of the separate entity of Manipur. Yangmasho Shaiza, another charismatic leader from Ukhrul joined the Manipur Nationalist Party which demanded the revocation of the Merger Agreement and the independence of Manipur.

Deprival of the tribal people of their democratic rights as given under the Manipur State Constitution Act, 1947 (along with other people of Manipur) led to several fallouts. Some sections of the tribal were pacified by the Chief Commissioner's administration by giving them official jobs. But when R. Suisa came into the political scene as an M.P. from Outer Manipur in 1957, he started to organise the Nagas of Manipur into a political party known as the Manipur Nega council which facilited the participation of Manipur Nagas in Phizo's Naga Nationalist movement. He and the his Secretary, Z. Ramyo and other protege Th. Muivah joined the NNC while merger had ceased to be a issue in Manipur politics. The creation of the Merger namely the Central rule in Manipur did not have any democratic base and it created a political vacuum in the hills of Manipur. Naturally, the Nagas joined in the Naga nationalist movement. However, the moderate elements among them, including the Congress and Socialist, both Naga and Kuki participated in the political movement for democracy leading to the establishment of the Territorial Council (1957) and Territorial Assembly (1963) and full statehood (1972).

## Conclusion

While there was no immediate ethnic response to the Merger, the Central Government's colonial attitude towards Manipur during the long central rule (1949-71) was the major cause of the political turmoils, economic backwardness and social tension in the hills of Manipur. Though 'if' in history is a wishful thinking, none can deny the fact that had there been no merger of Manipur in a crude and imperialistic manner, reminiscent of the British conquest of Manipur in 1891, and had the autonomy under the Manipur State Constitution Act been allowed to continue without interference from India, the painful course of history of the last 44 years would have been different. But Merger is now a fait accompli.

CHAPTER THIRTEEN

# RECURRENCE OF HISTORICAL FORCES

## Insurgency in Manipur, 1981

Revolts and rebellions occurred in Manipur in the 20th century at almost regular intervals; anti-British tribal uprisings like the **Kuki Rebellion** 1917-19, the **Zeliangrong Naga Uprising** 1930-32 and the **anti-feudal and anti-monopolist Nupilal**; the **Great Women Agitation** of 1939-40 broke out in the colonial period; and after independence, revolutionary movement like the **Communist Revolt of Hijam Irabot** (1948-51), the **Naga Rebellion** (since *1958)* and **Kuki Mizo Rebellion** (since 1966) are still fresh and very much contemporaneous. These insurgencies with their varying degrees of success or failure reflected the aspirations of the three major ethnic groups of the state, namely, the Meitei of Imphal Valley, the Nagas and Kuki-Mizos of the surrounding hills. The Pre-independence tribal uprisings were anti-imperialist tribal based. The Great Women Agitation was not only anti-monopolistic but it was for democratic constitutional reforms and it was influenced by the Indian Nationalist struggle for freedom. The post independence movements like that of the Nagas and Kuki-Mizos are more or less nationalist and aimed at the establishment of sovereign Naga, Kuki and Mizo states as a part of bigger Nagaland and Mizoram. The revolt in the Imphal Valley 1948-51 was also based on Meitei nationalism with communist ideological orientation. It was a peasant revolt for the establishment of a sovereign Manipur and thus contrary to the enthusiastic pro-India Congress movement for merger of the state with India Union by abolishing monarchy.

There were three schools of political opinions in Manipur at the time of the merger of the state with India on 15th October, 1949. The peasant revolutionaries under the leadership of Irabot were fighting for the establishment of a sovereign Socialist republic in Manipur and some areas of Upper Burma; the urban elitist Congress leaders wanted integration with India as they were greatly influenced by Indian nationalism projected through the personalities of Mahatma Gandhi, Nehru and Subash. The third group, very meek and silent were the Meitei nationalists who wanted to retain an independent status of Manipur with a very vague idea of treaty relation with India. The movement for integration with India sponsored by the urban elitist. Indian Nationalists succeeded while the red revolt failed; the Meitei nationalists remained silent and sulky.

The present insurgency is not a direct continuation of the earlier revolts but its historical roots are engrained in them. The Communist ideology and Meitei Nationalism are behind the insurgencies then and now. In the late sixties, the **Revolutionary Government of Manipur** (RGM) was formed by some educated revolutionary youths with assistance from some tribal leaders. It was at a time when the people of Manipur, put under the central administration (Union Territory), were politically frustrated with India, and were struggling for political freedom either inside Indian Union or outside. Statehood for Manipur, long denied to her on the pretext of economic non-availability was demanded by the political parties. The RGM and the revolutionary groups were however faction ridden and the conflicts in leadership surfaced when their leaders went to East Pakistan for training in guerilla warfare and arms. The police cracked down on their leaders at Imphal and many of the revolutionary youths were arrested at the India Pakistan borders and lodged at Tripura jail. After the liberation of Bangladesh, the RGM personnel returned to Manipur and were arrested after several encounters at the Assam, Manipur border. By 1972, the RGM was suppressed; either their leaders were in Manipur or Tripura Jails or inactive. In 1972, statehood was granted to Manipur and a popular ministry installed thereafter granted partial amnesty and a few years after, the Government of Manipur granted a universal amnesty. Thus by 1975, all the revolutionaries were released and rehabilitation works were taken up.

However, the revolutionary experience with the RGM and their amnesty produced three groups: the Manipuri nationalists and the Marxists; the nationalists were further divided into moderates and activists.

The RGM members in Tripura jail become converts to Marxism Leninism as a result of their contact with the Naxalites here. Of the nationalists group, the moderates withdrew from the scene. The activists came to be associated with the then Chief Minister of Manipur, R.K. Dorendra Singh. The former RGM activists' support to his ministry had destroyed the independent credibility of the former. This was strongly opposed by the Marxist oriented Tripura returned RGM activists. The two groups parted ways. It was a crucial point in the movement ideologically and strategically. The revolutionary attempts were based on Manipur nationalism which covers both the Meitei of valley and hill tribes; their source of help was non-communist country, Pakistan. But after the 1975 splits, the more extreme group was Maoist oriented and China became their source of help and aspiration. In the struggle for leadership, the nationalist group led by O. Shudirkumar was greatly weakened after his assassination and the Maoist group led by N. Bisheswar, the Lhasa trained leader emerged as the successful group. The **People's Liberation Army** (PLA) Eastern Region was formed and the Revolutionary Government of Manipur was abolished by his successful group. Almost simultaneously, another group known as the **People's Revolutionary Party of Kangleipak** (PREPAK) was formed in the valley. They also claim to be Marxist revolutionary. The Prepak was broken up into several factions: R.K. Tulachandra group, Maipak Sharma group etc. The PLA is now dominating the whole revolutionary scene in Manipur valley.

### Deep rooted urban phenomenon

The insurgency in Manipur valley initially is an urban phenomenon. The insurgents are mostly urban youths who get active support from the urban middle classes and the intellectuals with a wide mass sympathy. This complex phenomenon of revolutionary situation is a product of deep rooted and intricate factors like, the crisis of identity, weakness of Indian political system, economic exploitation, bureaucratic corruption, unemployment of youths and influence of foreign power and ideology.

The crisis of identity or fear of losing it through which Manipur is passing through is reflected in different forms. The myth of the Aryan origin of the Meitei , which was created by the Brahmanical scholars after their conversion into Hinduism in the 18th century has now been exploded. The confusion between race, language, culture and Hindu religion led the people to think that their profession of Hinduism made them Aryans. The Meiteis are racially and linguistically Tibeto-Burmans with Tai and some Aryan admixtures due to immigration from different regions in different periods of history. The myth of Aryan connection which provided a strong base for belonging to Hindu world of India was questioned first by the Sanamahi cult; the pre-Hindu Meitei religion. This move was in the early stage against the Brahmin exploitation and advocated the preservation and promotion of the racial and cultural identity of the Meitei.

The Sanamahi cult revived the Meitei script, old literature and contributed greatly to the reassertion of the distinct Meitei identity. This movement turns out to be at later stage anti-Hindu and to some extent anti outsider. This assertion of identity in political system means sovereignty of Manipur, the Meitei cultural tradition and separateness of Manipur from the rest of India. This psychological feeling influenced some people to seek a new political system as an alternative to Indian democratic system. One Sanamahi scholar rationalises that even the Maoist inclination of the insurgents is a reaction against the Indian system and represents an alternative to it, as a part of assertion of the Meitei identity. The Meitei nationalism has been simultaneously aroused. The words Manipur and Manipuri are losing their meaning and gradually being replaced by Kangleipak and Meitei respectively. The name of Kangleipak has been universally adopted by the revolutionary groups. It is strongly felt that the Meitei identity can only be preserved and fostered in a Meitei sovereign state which is of course in a strict geographical sense the 700 sq. miles Imphal valley, the homeland of the Meiteis. The fear of being swallowed up by the great Indian multitude due to the influx immigrants from outside causing immense demographic imbalance and thus causing the loss of cultural identity of the people is strongly felt by every section of the society. The intense search for self identity has created a danger of atominization of the social fabric of Manipur. This is the strongest motivation factor in the revival of the Meitei nationalism.

It is an irony that the urban elite of Manipur who was

the most vociferous group in 1949 to merge with Indian Union, thirty years later, is disenchanted with the Indian political system. This frustration is due to the Indian apathy to the political aspirations of the people of Manipur. In 1949, the people did not like the feudalistic monarchy of the king and wanted to enjoy the democratic rights and privileges of free country like India. But instead of giving the same political right guaranteed by the Indian constitution, Manipur was put under the central administration for 23 years (1949-1972). The central rule with its bureaucratic set up produced an adverse affect on the people. The people who were ruled by their own king with a democratic constitution between 1947-49 were denied all the democratic rights. No responsible form of Government was granted on the pretext of the lack of democratic experience, Attempts were made to destroy the political entity of Manipur; the States Reorganisation Commission went to the extent of recommending the merger of Manipur into Assam by forming a district therein. This was prevented by the personal intervention of Prime Minister Jawaharlal Nehru. Again statehood was denied to Manipur on the alleged ground of economic non-viability, though the Government of India granted statehood to Nagaland as early as 1963 despite its economic deficiencies. These leaders and parties who fought for merger with India were in an embarased position. If the democratic right and privileges which are enjoyed by fellow citizens are denied to the people of Manipur, a natural question is raised, whether such an association with India will be helpful to them. People had started interpreting the long central administration under Chief Commissioner and Lt. Governor as the Indian version of colonial rule. Enough damage was done during this period of central administration and the politically nationalist minded youths seriously questioned the benefits of political association with India, and the manner of pressurisation on the Maharaja of Manipur to sign the Merger Agreement in 1949 was dug up for public discussions. The revolutionary youths wanted to establish an independent state of Manipur. Statehood, of course, was granted in 1972 but enough frustration and bitterness were created. Moreover the working of the democratic institutions like the Union Territorial Council, later on Legislative Assembly were so limited that they could not meet the rising aspirations of the people. Even after statehood, despite the great central assistance, the performance of the parliamentary system in the state is not a happy experience. The weakness of the political system has been exploited to magnify the failure of the democratic system. Thus most of the ills of Manipur could be attributed to the inordinately long central rule; this does not absolve the failure of the political rulers after statehood. Both of them are responsible for the present situation.

To the political frustrations of the people are added the miseries of economic stagnancy and exploitation by an unholy alliance between the big business, corrupt bureaucracy and pliant political leadership which is equally corrupt and inefficient. The huge fund allocations in the Government budget have gone to the contractors and big business. The emergence of an affluent class of contractors, engineers and big business is a disturbing social phenomenon in Manipur. Their involvement in politics specially during ministry making has commercialised the whole political process in the state. There is one instance of one contractor participating in a Cabinet meeting. There is no industrial development worth to name; there is no productivity. It is a consumer oriented economy; goods are supplied from outside and naturally money is again drained away. Like elsewhere, the educated unemployment is increasing. The unemployment of the youths with bureaucratic non-concern could be taken as an important direct cause of the involvement of the youth in the present insurgency. The leaders of the insurgency and many of their followers have been victims of bureaucratic apathy and corruption and one naturally feels that the failure to provide social and economic justice to the people, especially the youths has led to the deterioration of the situation and strengthening of the hands of the insurgents to carry on their activities. As there is no industry in Manipur, the Government is the greatest employer and corruption is rampant, jobs are given to the highest bidders. One institution which is responsible for insurgency is the corrupt bureaucracy. But it is interesting to note that the bureaucracy does not have a will to meet the challenges of insurgency but some sections of the urban bureaucracy are supporting the insurgency mostly on personal grounds and to show off their influence among them. But administrative corruptions continue to flourish without fear, And so long this is not checked or at least minimised, there will be no salvation for Manipur.

A social factor which is to be taken note of is the feeling of xenophobia which is the result of long central bureaucratic rule and economic exploitation. The administration was manned by officers sent from Delhi, the whole economy is in the hands of few monopoly houses, all outsiders, of Imphal; this naturally leads to an anti-outsider feeling. It is found that inspite of Hinduism, the racial difference is greatly felt by the people of Manipur whenever they go to other parts of India. This is strongly felt by the students reading throughout the country. When they get such an experience in an impressionable age a social apathy has been developed. It is a dangerous trend which has been exploited by the insurgents. The popular myth that religious identity will ensure the unity of the country is exploded in Manipur. Christian missions have been blamed for troubles in North east and it is suggested Hindu missions will ensure the integrity of the India. But in Manipur valley, the converted Hindu Meiteis do no longer hold such a view. Hinduism cannot be equated with Indian nationalism.

In such a situation Marxism-Leninism came in as a handy weapon for curing the ills of society. The insurgents have found an ideology and method which are anticapitalist, anti parliamentary system, anti Indian, and China became their inspirer if not the actual aid giver.

**Objective**

The objective of the PLA appears to be quite broad, not confined to Manipur alone. They are building up a revolutionary front for liberation of Manipur valley in collaboration with other revolutionary groups working in other parts of North East India and Upper Bunna. The PREPAK aim at the establishment of a revolutionary government in Manipur but in operational terms Kangleipak. Other is the Kangleipak Communist Party (KCP) more or less on PREPAK line. Prepak has been greatly weakened. The leadership of the PLA appears to be ideologically clear and mature.

The insurgents have resorted to urban guerilla warfare and it is believed that they have infiltrated in all branches of administration. Their attacks on security forces are quite daring. Their propaganda with pamphlets, wall writings, even balloons appear to be quite affective. Two years ago, the civil government was demoralised and could not face the insurgents. With the moving in of the Army the will to resist has been restored. The counter insurgency measures so far appear to be quite successful. The PREPAK is almost liquidated. The military operations, curfew, firing, death, looting of banks and shops have become usual feature of life at Imphal. It is true that the insurgency is not a mere law and order problem. It has to be tackled at the political, economic, social and administrative levels also. The political leadership of the state is expected to play a more positive role in solving the issue. The army will be a help and not the final solution to insurgency.

The ideological reply is to be provided by the leadership which stands for Indian nationalism and administrative frame work is to be provided by the Government.

CHAPTER FOURTEEN

# MODERNIZATION AS A HISTORICAL PROCESS

## Modernization of Tribal Society

The tribal Society in Manipur came into contact with modern civilization only with the British conquest and their colonial rule over Manipur for about half a century. The contact with the European and their administration resulted into a process of social change in Manipur including the tribes. This change has been further accentuated after the massive economic development programmes after India's independence. This process of social and economic transformation has been described by sociologists either as modernisation or westernisation. M.N. Srinivas prefers to call it westernisation. He writes, "westernisation is used to characterise the changes brought about in Indian society and culture as a result of 150 years of British rule and the term subsumes changes occurring different levels: technology, institutions, ideology and values" (Srinivas : 1972). He further writes, "There is a need for such a term when analysing changes that non-western society undergoes as a result of prolonged contact with a western one". Since the tribes of Manipur had comparatively shorter period of contacts with the British, 56 years to be exact, but having been brought into intimate contacts with India and things Indian, it will not be appropriate to apply this term to this aspect of social change among the tribes of Manipur. According to Wilbert Moore, "Modernization is a total transformation of a traditional or a premodern society into the types of technology and associated social organisation that characterise the 'advanced' economically prosperous and relatively stable political nature of the western world (Moore, 1975). Thus modernisation means the process of sociocultural change whereby less developed societies acquire characteristics common to more developed societies. But in the tribal world, modernization is meant to develop the economy of the tribal society upto the subsistence level with certain amount of developed technologies and modification of some cultural aspects suitably adaptable to that new society (Bhadra: 1975). An aspect of this social transformation, namely the process of the transfer of cultural and social elements from one society to another, in case of tribes of Manipur, from European or Indian society to tribal society is also called acculturation which is associated with modernization. The catalysing agents of such acculturation are imperialism including colonization, and indirect rule, conquest and military occupation, religious imperialism (missionary religion) mass migration, individual migration, economic trade, tourism, imported labour, transfer of knowledge, diplomacy, etc. And the items of acculturation are usually tools and technologies, forms of-social organization, legal codes and system of religious beliefs.

Applying this criteria to tribal Manipur, we find out that the tribes had adopted European technologies, legal codes introduced by the Government and a foreign religion introduced by the European, namely Christianity. To put it in another way, the British Rule in hill areas of Manipur produced great changes in tribal society and economy as the result of the adoption of the following:

(i) New Technology introduced by the British.

(ii) New Institutions introduced in the administration.

(iii) Western Education.

(iv) Beliefs and values, meaning Christianity and liberal western political ideas.

The new technology, the administrative and legal system and Christianity continue to develop further after Manipur's merger with Indian Union and influence the process of transformation of tribal society in Manipur.

This paper is concerned with the problem of modernization with regard to technological and institutional changes that were introduced in the hill areas of Manipur and their consequences in the body politic of tribal Manipur both in the colonial and post-independence periods.

The hill tribes of Manipur, both Nagas and Kuki-Chins, almost upto the middle of 20th century were living in their self-sufficient villages with their community ownership of land and forests and political economy. In most cases, the tribal village even today is more than a collection of individuals; it is a social group (preferably a kinship group), a self-sufficient economic unit, a cultural pattern, a religious society with more or less political autonomy. What Karl Marx wrote about the traditional Indian village in middle of the 19th century is equally true of the tribal villages. Marx writes, "Their family communities were based on domestic industry, in that peculiar combination of hand weaving, hand spinning and hand tilling agriculture which gave the self supporting power" (Marx :1858). Traditional tribal society is a village society. In Manipur hills, W. McCulloch described some of the tribal villages in 1859 as independent village republics (McCulloch : 1859) other colonial accounts and anthropological writings ranging from Pemberton to Hodson, from Shakespear to Shaw have described the tribal village society more or less in the similar way.

The new technology which the Europeans brought to Manipur and the institutional changes, especially in administration namely, introduction of revenue, regulation of land ownership system, forest regulation, legal system, education and ideologies including Christian religion as stated earlier have brought great changes in tribal society. The traditional tribal society with its primitive technology for productive activities has been exposed to the outside world. It produced reactions amongst the tribes of Manipur; one was peaceful revolution in religion, education, economic development, inculcation of European liberal ideology of democracy and the other was a resistance against colonial political domination taking the form of social and political movements like Kuki Rebellion, Zeliangrong Movement of Jodonang and Gaidinliu which were anti-imperialistic. And later on ethnic political movements like the Naga, Kuki-Mizo movements, occurred in the post Independence era.

## Technological change

Technology is the most important criteria of measuring the standard of a civilization. Technology implies tools and implements, and manners of its organisation. It is directly linked up with economic organisation of production relation; the division of labour among men, women and children. Everyone of each category is engaged in production activities, in cultivation and housekeeping, family and community life. The tribal technology is still primitive; traditional tools and implements used by them are daos, hoe and axe, But technological change is a fundamental vehicle of change in; human society and economy; at the same time it is a very old process. As Margaret Mead observes, technical change is also as old as civilization and since time immemorial, the ways of the life of the whole people have been transformed by the introduction of new tools and new technical procedure such as inventions like the plough, the domestication of animals, writing and use of steams.

Manipur's search for an improved military technology in 18th and19th century led her to an alliance with the British which provided the latest European military technology during the First Anglo-Burmese War 1824-26. Since then Manipur gradually, but with great caution started accepting European technology in communication, postal system later on telegraphy (1886). The Maharajahs initially objected to introduction of telegraph lines. After British conquest, the flow of communication, telegraphy wireless, printing press, construction of improved roads and mechanised means of transport (cycle, motor vehicles etc.) introduction of electric power, modern medicine and modern health services, water supply and civil engineering constitute the new technology. Further during the 2nd World War, Manipur was exposed to the latest European technology, mostly destructive technology; military machines, telephone, air transport and tremendous improvement in transportation system. Later on, the Government of India had brought the technology further into the interior of the tribal areas. And the tribal people have responded to the use and utilization of the new technology. Their standard of living has been improved, scientific tools and implements are used for domestic purposes, improved utensils, radio, transmitter etc. Westernization has set in the tribal society contributing to the emergence of an elite. The new technology has facilitated the administration tremendously.

But unfortunately, modernization has not set in their productive activities neither in agriculture nor in cottage industries. The scientific technology has not affected the productive system much except in some urban growth centres like Churachandpur.

The people still excel in heavy and relatively crude type of works, precision and finesse are not yet their speciality, village industries are confined to handicrafts, weaving and cane and bamboo works. Their agricultural technology in most areas either in Jhum or terrace Cultivation is still primitive, the hoe is still the most formidable implement. However in big river valleys, like the Khuga basin in South District, Khoupum valley, upper reaches of Imphal and Barak river basin the plough has come; even power tillers and tractors have appeared in the scene. They are mere symbols of the willingness of the people to adapt to the new agriculture technology, rather than real change. Their non agricultural skills are confined to house building, handicrafts; weaving and basketry, the dao, the axe and the hoe are still indispensable weapons.

But motivation for change is already there; the massive industrialization boost given by the Government training of artisans, introduction of village industries have prepared the ground for change in outlook. For example the rice mill in the tribal villages driven by diesel has given a great relief to the womenfolk in saving their labour and time for use in production purpose. These technological changes both at the higher level, say in the macro level and village level have contributed to the transformation of the tribal society.

## Institutional change

The tribal villages in the pre-English period were a sort of autonomous_republics with minimum interference from the kings of Manipur except some symbolic political control. With the introduction of British rule in Manipur in 1891, the hill tribes were brought under the direct British administration. The British administration in Manipur as elsewhere concentrated on the survey of the land, settlement of land revenues, in case of Manipur hills, introduction of hill house tax, maintenance of police and during war, army, creating a bureaucracy to carry on their administration; instituting law courts, codifying the laws, (in Manipur hills, they accepted tribal customary laws which dealt with civil case) development of minimum communication for carrying on their administration, like post and telegraph, construction of road and bridge paths, establishment of a few primary schools to provide four grade employees, opening of a printing press (publication of books for schools in local language greatly facilitated spread of primary education) and spread of Christianity by encouraging and supporting the Christian missionaries.

Over and above the technological changes introduced by the British administration and Christianity brought a more fundamental change in tribal society. After India's independence, more fundamental institutional changes have been introduced as a result of the democratic form of Government. The successive Governments after the British: Manipur State 1947- 49, part -C State, 1949-55 : Union Territory 1967-1971, statehood since 1972, introduction of Village Authorities Act, 1956, the Autonomous District Councils have facilitated the participation of the representatives of the tribal people in the process of decision making, it is one of the direct fruits of Indian democracy.

Since independence, education has tremendously developed. The educated tribal young men had entered all levels of the bureaucracy even in the specialised branches of administration like, medical, public works, agricultural and horticulture and forestry.

With the intensification of the administration establishment of district courts, district level departments the tribes have started feeling the pinch of administration also. The forest regulation is giving them headache as the Government policy challenges their traditional community ownership and control over village land and forests. The working of the village

Village Authority which is modelled to function as a law court is in doldrums. It is also to be remodelled to function as an agency for developmental work in the villages.

These institutional changes which are direct outcome of Indian democratic system ought to be studied in greater depth. These changes are the foundation of modernization. The liberal ideas of democracy, individual liberty, human rights and common good of the community are to be blended with traditional tribal values and ethos.

## Political consequences

The introduction of direct British rule in hill areas of Manipur, especially the introduction of hill house tax of Rs. 3/- per annum (now increased Rs. 15/-) rendering of forced labour and direct adjudication of tribal customary cases disturbed the agriculture oriented tribal society based on barter economy. The British policy on forest to serve their commercial interests was in direct contrast to the tribal community interest. The settlement of different tribal communities side by side as a part of their control over the hill tribes based on divide and rule policy created an endless struggle for control over jhum land, thus creating a distance between the indigenous hill tribes and the administration. The exploitative stance of the petty colonial administrators was resented by the hill tribes. Only those hill tribes among whom, the Christian missionaries worked were favoured and there was better equation between them and the Government. The British rule with its associated practices directly affected the tribal love for freedom. Thus the political consequences of the new technology and British administration were protest movements of which the Kuki rebellion and Zeliangrong movement of Jadongnang and Gaidinliu 1927-32 are the best examples. Inspite of these uprisings, Christian mission and colonial administration produced a tribal elite who manned the lower level of bureaucracy and gave support to the administration. During the 2nd World Wa except among a few individuals, the tribal people gave support to the British during the epic fight against the Japanese invaders.

However after India's independence and merger of Manipur with Indian union, educational development and participation in the democratic process of decision making bodies like, state legislature and national parliament have made the tribal fully conscious of the need for further progress. The gap between the expectation and fulfilment of their aspiration is still very wide. The political leadership is provided by a tribal elite who protects the interest of the tribal bureaucracy, business and capitalist groups. Though class formation has not started in tribal society, the emergence of the contractors as an exploiting group is the most disturbing feature of tribal society in their march towards modernisation. We need not go into the causes of such a phenomenon at this stage.

Then, the participation in Indian democracy made the tribal come into contact with the ideas of nationalism, secularism, democracy and socialism. Though there is a general appreciation for these universal ideas adopted by India, the lurking fear of the great Indian multitude is so strong that the search for ethnic identity among the hill tribes a political force in the transformation of tribal society; there are contradictory forces at work. While there is an urge to identify with greater Naga personality, (some say nationality) and Kuki-Mizo identity, the individual tribes are working to keep their individual tribal identifies at any cost. So one of the political movement and the demand for ethnic homelands, Ethnic politics has come even to the valley of Manipur where Indian nationalist forces are at work for a long time.

Another consequence is the politiazation of tribal culture as in the case of the Mizo as B.B. Goswami has highlighted. This has been adopted as a part of ethnic movement. The working of the democratic institutions especially the election of legislative bodies, District Council and Village authorities have created schism in the traditional tribal leadership at the village, clan and tribe levels. Instead of territorial or party loyalties, clan and family loyalties are given greater importance. Just like caste being a factor in Hindu majority states, clan is emerging as a factor in tribal politics which is an undesirable element.

## REFERENCES

1. M.N. Srinivas, *Social change in Modem India,* 1972.
2. Wilbert Moore, *Social Change,* 1975.
3. R.K. Bhadra, *India Tribes and Modernization,* 1975, North Eastern bulletin.
4. A.B. Shah, and C.R.M. Rao, *Tradition and Modernity in India,* 1965, Delhi.
5. W. McCulloch, *An account of the Valley of Munnipore,* 1859, Calcutta.

CHAPTER FIFTEEN

# CRISIS OF IDENTITY IN MANIPUR

## Identity and Identity Crisis

The terms, identity and identity crisis require some conceptual clarifications. Identity is the state or fact of remaining the same one or ones, under varying conditions or circumstances. Identity is, therefore, the feeling that we as individuals are the same persons as we were yesterday and last year. To Eric H. Erikson, identity "is the sense of sameness and continuity" of an individual or a group. Identity, thus, is a psycho-social phenomenon; it may be the feeling of an individual or group that his or their past (memories or history purposes and values, experience and belief in a future belong to him or them) With this view, we talk of social identity, ethnic or cultural identity of communities or nations. For example, the social identity of an ethnic group includes their common past or history, cultural heritage linguistic affinity, their shared experiences, struggle and suffering, with a strong sense of belonging to each other and or identification with an ideology and a belief in the common future. Identity is the experience of the individual or group as recongnizable, continuous and persistent identity. Identity is what one thinks about himself as the real "ME".

Identity crisis means an acute anxiety state experienced by a person or group who finds it difficult to establish a clearly defined personal or group identity. Whenever there occurs a phase or period seeking new set of definition amidst unclear role choices of an individual or group, there occurs the psycho-social phenomenon of identity crisis. To Erikson, "Crisis means a crucial time or an inescapable turning point for better or worse". Better' means a confluence of the constructive energies of an individual or society' and worse means a prolonged identity confusion in young individuals and society. Therefore, identity crisis is a recurring phenomenon in the social development of a group or community. In every new generation, there is always a demand for identity. A society has to respond to these demands and confirm positive identity to regenerate itself and preserve. Such psycho-social phenomenon also has occurred in the social situation of Manipur.

## Ethnic Pluralism and Identity Crisis

Manipur is a plural society with three ethnic groups, the Meiteis, Nagas and Kukis as major constituents of her population. Different ethnic, social, linguistic and cultural groups always strive to maintain and preserve their identity which assumes different forms and manifestations depending on the need of the groups concerned, politico~ethnic, linguistic, cultural and religious. This phenomenon in all aspects exists in Manipur making the identity crisis more complex. And the ethnic pluralism is the root cause of the absence of the common identity of the people of Manipur. However, the genesis of the identity crisis can be traced to the Sanskritization of Manipur, British colonialism, Christian evangelism among the hill tribes, Manipur's merger into Indian Union and occurrence of tribal solidarity movements.

Historically speaking, Manipur has been the meeting

place of different races, languages and religions. Imphal valley which is on the trade and migration routes between India and South East Asia is a cradle of civilization. The valley is the habitat of the Meiteis, the dominant group; and the hill tribes, the Nagas and the Kuki Chins live in the surrounding hills. The process of the evolution of the Meitei state and society took more than one thousand years in the Imphal valley to take the present form. The Meitei society is a kinship based society. They are divided into seven salais (clan), namely, Ningthouja (Mangang), Khuman, Luwang, Angom, Moirang, Kha-Nganba and Sarang Leishangthem. These clans were once distinct social entities before they were integrated socially after political subjugation and assuming the status of clan. Emergence of the Meitei nationality with Meitei language, Meitei political supremacy, and Meitei salai system constitutes a unique historical phenomenon. Anthropological and linguistic studies clearly point out that the Meiteis are Tibeto Bunnan ethnically and linguistically while the Aryan and Tai elements have also been absorbed in the process of the evolution of the Meitei society. With the conversion of the royalty and people of Manipur into Hinduism in the eighteenth century, the sanskritization of the Meitei state and society was set rolling; deliberate attempts were made to give a new identity to the people and kingdom of Manipur. The kingdom was renamed 'Manipur' according to the Sanamahi Laikan in 1724 A.D. A new genealogy of the royal family was prepared tracing its origin to the Pandava hero, Arjuna of the Mahabharata claiming an Aryan origin of the Meities who were classified as the Kshatriya caste. And a religious syncretism between traditional Meitei religion with Hinduism was brought about. The sanskritization process created a confusion due to the identification of religion with racial or ethnic origin. From the eighteenth to the middle of the twentieth century, persistent efforts were made by the court's Brahmin scholars to prove the Aryan origin of the Meiteis despite the European scholars' rational view that they are Tibeto

Burman of the Mongoloid stock. The Meiteis have undergone an identity crisis for the last two and half centuries.

The hill tribes who occupy the periphereal mountains have racial affinity, but culturally and technologically, the lag behind and are confined to their village level society. During the pre-British period they were known by different tribal names. But during the British colonial rule, they were broadly categorised for administrative convenience into Naga tribes and Kuki tribes. The two constellations of tribal identity with Naga and Kuki is a result of British colonialism. Moreover, Christianity was introduced among these tribes. So the dichotomy which was already there during the pre-colonial days into the Hindu Meiteis and hill tribes was sharpened with the externally imposed identity of Christianised Nagas and Kukis. The ethnic pluralism on the basis of the three entities, Meitei, Naga and Kuki has prevented the emergence of the common identity of the people of Manipur.

## Tribal Identity expansion Movement

The colonial government's arbitrary classification was responsible for dividing the hill tribes into Naga and Kuki. This classification led to ethnic identification of the tribes into these two constellations. However identification with the Naga has been a process of Pan-Naga identity. This ethnic identification of tribes into Naga constellation may be called a process of Nagaisation which has social cultural and political implications. The Nagaisation process was greatly strengthened by the Naga insurgency for independence based on loose form of Naga nationalism. Now Nagas are more or less regarded as an emerging nationality. Within the broad Naga constellation, there are several tribal solidarity process. Among the Tangkhuls who have dialectical difference for almost every village, the adoption of Ukhrul dialect as the standard Tangkhul literary language has strengthened the Tangkhul identity and unity. The Zemi, Liangmei, Rongmei and Puime also started the Zeliangrong movement to forge unity and promote integration among these cognate tribes. A Zeliangrong identity has now been formed. During the post independence period, the Anals, Moyon, Monshang and Lamgang tribes organised the 'Pakan' movement to bring the four tribes under one common name "Pakan" but it failed. The Moyon and Monshang tribes tried to combine into "Mon" but the sperate feeling of Moyon and Monshang is still very strong.

The Kom-Rem movement was also organised with a view to bringing the Kom, Chiru, Aimol, Purum and at one time the Koireng to give a common identity to these tribes. The Mao-Maram tribal alliance for political purpose has not led to social or cultural integration. The Poumei group does not like to be grouped with Mao tribe. Poumei has been recognised as a separate tribe in 2003.

Among the Kukis there is no such process of integration till the Mizo insurgency. While Kuki Rebellion (1917-1919) was aimed at Kuki "independence", it did not lead to further integration but to separation into distinct tribes. But the Mizo integration movement again restored a sense of unity among the Kukis and Mizo. The concept of the Kuki-Mizo was popularised. Now it is being replaced by the Zomi movement after the solution of the Mizo rebellion. The Zo or Zomi identity is again catching on among the Kuki-Chin tribes of Manipur and surrounding areas, though tribal identities have not been submerged under it. The Chin-Kuki-Mizo solidarity process is continuing while the Thadous are asserting their Kuki identity.

## Crisis of Meitei identity

The identity of the Meiteis is a very controversial issue. The Aryan origin of the Meiteis was successfully challenged and the myth has now been exploded. This is a result of the

Meitei cultural revivalism represented by the Sanamahi Movement initially and later on by scientifically oriented Meitei scholars on history, literature and anthropology. Though the Aryan origin has been rejected and the Tibeto-Burman identity based on ethnicity and linguistics has been accepted, there are still scholars who believe in the Tai origin of the Meitei like the earlier Aryan origin of the Meiteis. This identity confusion persists because of the multiple ethnic roots of the Meitei nationality. The Meiteis are divided into three: **the MeiteiAriba** (indigenous Meitei), **Nongchup Haram** (those immigrants from the west) and the **Nongpok Haram** (the immigrants from the east). The western immigrants were Indo-Aryan, the eastern immigrants consisting of the Shans or Tai, Burmese and others were absorbed to Meitei society.

One important feature of the identity problem of the Meitei is that though they were a ruling group, they could not bring the hill tribes into their identity expansion canvass. Through sanskritization the king had adopted the name of Manipur. And Manipuri has been widely used to mean the Meiteis, Meitei language, literature, dance and music. The hill tribes are outside the connotation of the terms 'Manipuri' or 'Meitei.'

## Repercussions of the identity crisis

Though the racial or ethnic identity is well established about the Meiteis or the tribes, the problem of names remains complex as ever before, Now a serious and difficult problem arises as to the question "Who is a Manipuri?" The hill tribes do not call themselves as Manipuri nor the plainsmen (the Meitei) call them as such. The tribes prefer to call themselves as Naga or Kuki or Mizo or by their tribal names. Though "Manipuri" means the Meitei and Meitei language, a section of the Meiteis like to call themselves as Meitei or Meetei. If this tendency continues, it will logically lead to a situation that Manipur may become just a mere geographical expression and Manipuri as inhabitants of Manipur including Meitei, Naga, Kuki Mizo (Zomi) and Pangan (Manipuri Muslim). However it would depend on willingness of the people both of the hills and valley to accept their Manipuriness. But Manipuriness has not been completely accepted by every section. So identity crisis will persist till new definition of identities of the different social groups has been evolved.

## REFERENCES

1. Erik H. Erikson, "On Identity" in *International Encyclopaedia of Social Science.*
2. S. Lokendrajit, Identity and Identity Crisis: a case of Manipur, in *North East India History Association,* Pashighat, 1987, Shillong 1988.
3. Gangmumei Kabui, Problem of Identity in Manipur *Journal of Manipur Student's Association,* Delhi, 1978.

# BIBLIOGRAPHY


Acton, Lord, *Lectures on Modern History*, London, 1960,

Barnes, H.E., *A History of Historical Writings*, New York, 1963.

Bhattacharjee, J.B., ed. *Studies on the History of North East India*, Shillong, 1985. *Proceedings of the North East India History Association*, Kohima Sessirn, 1987.

Bloch, Marc, *Historian's Craft's*, London, 1953.

Braudel, Ferdinald, *On History*, London, 1986.

Bury, J.B., *The Idea of Progress: An Inquiry into its Origin and Growth*, New York, 1954.

Carr, E.H., *What is History?*, London, .1962.

Chakravarty, S., ed., *Social Science and Social Concern*. Mittals, New Delhi, 1993.

Collingwood, R.G., *Idea of History*, London, 1946.

Elton, G.R., *Political History,Principles and Practice*, New York, 1970. *Practice of History*, Collins, 1970.

Gardiner, Patrick, *Theories of History*, New York, 1969.

Goel, Dharmendra, *Philosophy of History*, Delhi, 1967.

Kabui, Gangmumei, *A History of Manipur, Pre-Colonial Period*, New Delhi, 1991.

Majumdar, R.K. and A.N. Srivastav, *Historiography*, Delhi, 1994.

N. Joykumar Singh, ed., *Proceedings of the Annual Session of Manipur Historical Society*, Imphal, 1995.

Sen, S.P.ed, *Historians and Historiography of Modern India*, Calcutta, 1973.

Spengler, Oswald, *The Decline of the West*, London, 1959.

Subramaniam, N., *Histo: iography*, Madras, 1974.

Toynbee, Arnold J., *A Study of History*, London, 1954. (Abridged versein).

Eric Hobsbawm, *On History*, London, 1997.

# INDEX